Practice in
French Grammar

for students starting post-16 courses

Second edition

Michael Gross

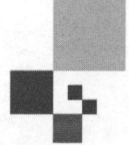 Nelson Thornes

First published in 1991 by:
Mary Glasgow Publications, an imprint of Stanley Thornes (Publishers) Ltd

Second edition 2001
Nelson Thornes Ltd
Delta Place
27 Bath Road
CHELTENHAM
GL53 7TH
United Kingdom

09 10 11 12 / 15 14 13 12 11 10

A catalogue record for this book is available from the British Library

ISBN 978 0 7487 6291 0

Illustrations by Jane Andrews
Page make-up by Tech-Set Ltd

Printed in China

Contents

Using this book   1

Glossary of grammatical terms   2

1 Finding your way   8

1.1 à + article + nouns   10
1.2 using **à** with distances   11
1.3 **de** + article + nouns   12
1.4 **en** + present participle   13
1.5 prepositions + infinitive   15
1.6 countries   17
1.7 the pronoun **en**   21
1.8 **en** and **dans** in expressions of time   23
1.9 numbers   24

2 Comparing the present and the past   26

2.1 the present tense   28
2.2 the present tense of reflexive verbs   38
2.3 the imperfect tense   39
2.4 savoir or pouvoir?   41
2.5 how to translate *in the morning, at the weekend, on Sundays* 41
2.6 the comparative form of adjectives   42
2.7 **le même... que** *(the same... as)*   44
2.8 how to translate *each other*   45

3 Talking about past experiences and expressing opinions   46

3.1 **des** or **de**?   48
3.2 the superlative   49
3.3 superlative + subjunctive   51
3.4 the relative pronouns **qui, que, dont**   52
3.5 how to translate *all, everybody, everything*   54
3.6 expressions of quantity + **de**   55
3.7 the perfect tense   57
3.8 **venir de** + infinitive   61
3.9 perfect or imperfect?   62

4   Talking about future plans and asking questions   64

4.1   the future tense   66
4.2   **quand** + future tense   68
4.3   the future perfect tense   70
4.4   nouns and adjectives + infinitive   71
4.5   verbs + inifinitive   73
4.6   question forms and question words   74
4.7   how to translate *what*   76
4.8   **ce** or **cela**?   78
4.9   how to talk about jobs   80

5   Giving advice and instructions   82

5.1   **demander à quelqu'un de faire**   84
5.2   **aider quelqu'un à faire**   86
5.3   the imperative   86
5.4   how to translate *after*   89
5.5   how to translate *before*   91
5.6   how to translate *ought to do/should do/ought to have
      done/should have done*   92
5.7   **dernier** and **prochain**   94
5.8   impersonal phrases: **il est** or **c'est**?   95
5.9   adverbs   98
5.10 the comparative and superlative of adverbs   101
5.11 **faire** + **infinitive** = *to have something done*   101
5.12 verbs + infinitive   101

6   Talking about people and things   104

6.1   expressing emotion using **quel**   106
6.2   direct object pronouns: **le, la, les**   107
6.3   direct and indirect object pronouns: **me, te, nous, vous**   109
6.4   indirect object pronouns **lui** and **leur**   111
6.5   **y** and **en**   112
6.6   the position of pronouns   113
6.7   pronouns used with prepositions **(chez moi, avec eux)**   116
6.8   pronouns used for emphasis   117
6.9   nouns + **à** + infinitive   118
6.10 possessive adjectives   119
6.11 possessive pronouns   123

6.12	agreement of adjectives	124
6.13	the irregular adjectives: **beau, nouveau, vieux**	127
6.14	how to translate *for* with expressions of time **(pendant, depuis, pour)**	129
6.15	using **c'est** and **ce sont** with things and people	130

7 Expressing choice and preference — 132

7.1	expressions of quantity and negatives + **de**	134
7.2	how to translate *a few, several, some*	137
7.3	**trop** and **assez**	138
7.4	the conditional tense	140
7.5	**si** clauses	142
7.6	**ce, cet, cette, ces**	144
7.7	**celui, celle, ceux, celles**	146
7.8	how to translate *which...?* and *which one?*	148

8 Making longer statements — 150

8.1	the pluperfect tense	152
8.2	the conditional perfect tense	154
8.3	how to translate *good, bad, well* and *badly*	154
8.4	how to translate *better*	155
8.5	how to use **on**	156
8.6	reflexive verbs (in the infinitive form)	157
8.7	expressions of emotion + subjunctive	158
8.8	to give someone something = **donner quelque chose à quelqu'un**	159
8.9	how to translate *such*	160
8.10	**personne ne..., rien ne...**	161
8.11	**quelque chose, quelqu'un, rien, personne + de**	161
8.12	direct and indirect speech	162

9 Being at the receiving end of and expressing negative reactions — 164

9.1	the passive	166
9.2	the negative	168
9.3	how to use **peut-être**	170
9.4	**rendre**	170
9.5	expressions of emotion + subjunctive	171
9.6	verbs + infinitive	172

10   An introduction to the subjunctive   174

10.1   uses of the subjunctive: general note   176
10.2   the present subjunctive   177
10.3   the perfect subjunctive   180
10.4   uses of the subjunctive: detailed practice   181

Appendices   186

1.   Prepositions   186
2.   Conjunctions   188
3.   The past historic   189

Solutions   190
Index   207

Using this book

Use this book to find out about or practise certain grammatical points that are causing you problems in your written or spoken French. You can also refer to a particular section of the book in order to plug a gap in your grammatical knowledge.

O   Use the index at the back of the book (pages 207–214) to find out where a particular structure is explained and practised.

O   Study the introductory dialogue or monologue to find out how the grammatical structure is used in a particular context. Use a dictionary to look up essential items of vocabulary.

O   Read the explanation of the grammatical rule in English and learn it thoroughly.

O   Then, even more important, learn by heart the French examples which use the structure.

O   Test your knowledge of the rule by doing the relevant exercises. As you do the exercises, write out the whole sentence or passage rather than just the item to be inserted, so that you can see the relationship between all the elements in the sentence.

O   Check your sentences from the correct version at the back of the book (pages 190–206). Pay particular attention to any that are wrong. Study the rules again and if you still cannot understand why your answer is wrong, consult your teacher.

O   Learn by heart the correct version of the sentences, noting their meanings as well as their form.

O   To consolidate your knowledge, translate the French sentences into English. After a few days, translate them back again into French, checking your translation with the original version.

O   Only learning by heart and frequent consolidation will enable you to master these structures fully so that you can use them competently in speech and in writing.

O   As you read more French, you will become aware of variations in the standard form of grammar that has been used in the dialogues and exercises in this book. Note these variations and discuss them with your teacher to see how you can begin to integrate these more flexible elements into your own writing and speaking.

Glossary of grammatical terms

Nouns

○ A noun is a word used to name a person or an object or an abstract quality:

a *tourist*	un **touriste**
a *campsite*	un **camping**
the *beauty* of the *scenery*	la **beauté** du **paysage**

○ Nouns can be used with the definite article (**the**) or the indefinite article (**a**). The French equivalents of **the** are **le**, **la**, **les** and of **a** are **un** and **une**.

○ In French nouns can be either masculine (le/un camping) or feminine (la/une plage). They can be used in the singular (a campsite, the campsite: un camping, le camping) or in the plural (some campers, the campers: des campeurs, les campeurs).

○ Most plurals end in **-s** but watch out for exceptions of the type below:

a. un château	des châteaux
un bateau	des bateaux
b. un animal	des animaux
un cheval	des chevaux
c. un caillou	des cailloux
un bijou	des bijoux

Pronouns

○ A pronoun is a word that can stand in for a noun, for example: **he, she, we, you, they, him, her, it**.

The guide escorted the tourists to the main square.
***He** escorted **them** to the main square.*
Le guide a emmené les touristes à la place principale.
Il les a emmenés à la place principale.

Adjectives

○ An adjective is a word used to describe a noun:

a *beautiful afternoon*	un **bel** après-midi
a *magnificent beach*	une plage **magnifique**

○ Possessive adjectives are words like **my, your, his, her, our, their** used with nouns to indicate possession:

my car	**ma** voiture
their villa	**leur** villa

○ Demonstrative adjectives are used to indicate which nouns are being talked about:

this house	**cette** maison
that restaurant	**ce** restaurant
these trees	**ces** arbres
those flowers	**ces** fleurs

○ The comparative form of the adjective is used when making comparisons between two people or things:

The hotel was more expensive than the other one but the pool was much smaller.
L'hôtel était **plus cher** que l'autre mais la piscine était beaucoup **plus petite**.

○ The superlative is used when comparing something or someone to two or more others.

the most attractive hotel	**le plus bel** hôtel
the best facilities	**les meilleurs** équipements
the least expensive room	la chambre **la moins chère**

A relative clause

○ A relative clause is a clause beginning with *who, which, that* or *where* which tells us more about a particular noun:

The family which had the pitch next to us was Dutch.
La famille **qui** avait l'emplacement à côté de nous était hollandaise.

The person or the thing that the relative clause refers back to is called the antecedent. In this example, the antecedent is the family (la famille).

○   In French, the relative pronoun is never omitted:

> *The museum we visited was very interesting.*
> Le musée **que** nous avons visité était très intéressant.

Verbs

○   A verb is a word which tells us what someone or something does or is or what someone thinks or feels:

> *Steve often goes to France.*   Steve **va** souvent en France.
> *He likes the good food.*   Il **aime** la bonne cuisine.
> *He speaks French reasonably*   Il **parle** assez bien le français.
> *well.*
> *He is a good windsurfer.*   C'**est** un bon véliplanchiste.

○   The verbs above are in the present tense because the emphasis is on what Steve is at the moment (a good windsurfer), what he generally likes about France (the good food) and what he often does (goes to France). Tenses indicate the time at which an event takes place. For example, if we talk about what Steve did last year, we use the past (perfect) tense:

> L'année dernière, Steve **a gagné** un concours.

If we talk about what he will do next year, we use the future tense:

> L'année prochaine, Steve **participera** à un concours à Paris.

○   Any verb can be either positive, indicating what someone does, or negative, indicating what someone doesn't do:

> Positive:
> *He watches a lot of T.V.*   Il **regarde** beaucoup la T.V.
>
> Negative:
> *He doesn't watch much T.V.*   Il **ne regarde pas** beaucoup la T.V.

Other negatives are: nothing (**ne... rien**), nobody (**ne... personne**), never (**ne... jamais**), no longer/no more (**ne... plus**).

○   The infinitive is the form of the verb used to name it, as in a dictionary, for example, *to go, to drink, to eat*: **aller, boire, manger**.

○ To conjugate a verb is to give the various parts of the verb corresponding to different persons of the verb, such as **I, you, he, she, we, they**. For example:

I go, you go, he goes, she goes, we go, they go
je vais, tu vas/vous allez, il va, elle va, nous allons, ils vont.

○ The subject of a verb is the person or thing that performs the action of that verb:

The tourists got into the coach. **Les touristes** sont montés dans le car.

The coach left for the airport. **Le car** est parti pour l'aéroport.

○ The direct object of the verb is the person or thing affected by the action of that verb:

The police arrested the campers because they had broken some windows.
Les agents ont arrêté **les campeurs** parce qu'ils avaient cassé des fenêtres.

○ The indirect object of the verb always conveys the idea of **to** somebody or something:

The man in charge spoke to the campers.
Le gardien a parlé **aux campeurs**.

○ The active form of the verb is used when the emphasis is on what the subject of the sentence does, whereas when the emphasis is on what is done to the subject of the sentence, the passive form of the verb is used:

Active form:
Steve pushed the French girl into the pool.
Steve **a poussé** la jeune Française dans la piscine.

Passive form:
Steve was pushed into the pool by a group of French boys.
Steve **a été poussé** dans la piscine par un groupe de jeunes Français.

5

○ The imperative form of the verb is used to give instructions and orders and to make suggestions:

> *Listen!* **Écoutez!**
> *Don't talk!* **Ne parlez pas!**
> *Let's go!* **Allons-y!**

○ A reflexive verb is a verb where the subject and object of the verb are the same person:

> *I hurt myself.* Je **me suis blessé(e)**.
> *They enjoyed themselves.* Ils **se sont bien amusés**.

○ The present participle is the part of the verb which ends in -ing in English and in -ant in French:

> *While jogging on the beach, he cut his foot.*
> **En faisant du footing** sur la plage, il s'est coupé le pied.

○ The past participle is that part of the verb that is used mainly to make up the perfect tense:

> *This year I've decided to go to Brittany.*
> Cette année, j'ai **décidé** d'aller en Bretagne.
> *I've often spent my holidays in France.*
> J'ai souvent **passé** mes vacances en France.

It is also used to form other compound tenses such as the pluperfect.

> *They had already booked a room in a hotel.*
> Ils **avaient** déjà **réservé** une chambre dans un hôtel.

Adverbs

○ An adverb is used mainly to tell us more about a verb, to indicate how an action is performed or when or where an action takes place:

> *Sometimes she plays very well.*
> **Quelquefois** elle joue très bien.
> *She runs everywhere all the time.*
> Elle court **tout le temps partout**.

Prepositions

○ A preposition is a word used in combination with a noun or pronoun to indicate where an action takes place or when it takes place or to give us more information about the circumstances in which it takes place:

> *During the holidays, we went to the beach with them every day until lunchtime. After lunch, in the cafeteria at the campsite, we went by car to visit interesting places not too far from the resort.*

> **Pendant** les vacances, nous allions **à** la plage **avec** eux tous les jours **jusqu'à** midi. **Après** le déjeuner, **dans** la cafétéria du camping, nous allions **en** voiture visiter des lieux d'intérêt pas trop **loin de** la station.

J'espère qu'on arrivera bientôt!

1 Finding your way

Grenoble, c'est loin?

A Grenoble hotel manager explains to a visiting Belgian businessman
how to get to the ski resort of l'Alpe-d'Huez.

M. Martens:	L'Alpe-d'Huez, c'est loin?	
Hôtelier:	Pas très loin. C'est **à une soixantaine de kilomètres d'ici, au sud-est de Grenoble**.	1.2 / 1.9 1.3
M. Martens:	Et on peut y aller en car?	
Hôtelier:	Mais oui, monsieur.	
M. Martens:	Et l'arrêt le plus proche, où est-il?	

Hôtelier:	Je ne sais pas exactement. Il vaudrait peut-être mieux aller **à la gare routière**. Ce serait plus facile.	1.1
M. Martens:	La gare routière, c'est loin d'ici?	
Hôtelier:	Allez jusqu'**au carrefour. Aux feux,** tournez à gauche, dans l'avenue Alsace-Lorraine, et vous arriverez directement **à la gare routière.** C'est **à environ 100 mètres, près de l'église.**	1.1 1.1 / 1.2 1.3
M. Martens:	Et **pour aller à l'Alpe-d'Huez,** on met combien de temps?	1.5 / 1.1
Hôtelier:	En voiture on y arrive **en 45 minutes** mais, **en prenant le car,** vous y arriverez **en une heure et demie.**	1.8 / 1.4 1.8
M. Martens:	Bon. Et la météo est bonne pour aujourd'hui?	
Hôtelier:	Oui. Aujourd'hui il va faire beau partout **dans le sud-est de la France.** Et l'Alpe-d'Huez est une station très ensoleillée. C'est une excellente station. Il y a toujours de la neige… Vous êtes bon skieur, monsieur? Vous faites souvent du ski?	1.6
M. Martens:	Pas vraiment. **J'en fais** de temps en temps. **J'en ai fait en Suisse** et en Autriche, mais jamais **en France. J'en fais** toutes les fois que **j'en ai** l'occasion.	1.7 1.6 1.7
Hôtelier:	Excusez-moi, monsieur, mais il faut penser **à l'heure.** Les cars, **il y en a seulement deux ou trois** le matin. Je crois qu'**il y en a un** à dix heures. Et il est déjà neuf heures et quart. Il part donc **dans trois quarts d'heure.**	1.1 1.7 1.8
M. Martens:	Bon. Encore un peu de café. Puis en route pour la gare routière et pour l'Alpe-d'Huez…	

1.1 *à* + article + nouns

au carrefour
à la gare routière
à l'Hôtel de Ville
aux feux

○ Note that **à** can mean *in, to,* and *at.* Look at these examples:

> M. Martens passe quatre jours **à** Grenoble.
> *M. Martens is spending four days in Grenoble.*

> Il vaudrait peut-être mieux aller **à la** gare routière.
> *It's probably best to go to the bus station.*

> **Aux** feux, tournez à gauche.
> *Turn left at the traffic lights.*

> Allez jusqu'**au** carrefour.
> *Go to the crossroads.*

○ Note that **à** changes form according to the article which follows. The rule is to use **à** in all cases except with **le** and **les,** when **à + le** becomes **au** and **à + les** becomes **aux**:

à + la → à la
à + l' → à l'
à + le → au
à + les → aux

>> Several tourists come into the tourist office in Grenoble: they want to know how to get to these places in town. Use **Pour aller...?** with the correct form of **à, à la, à l', au, aux,** to ask the way to each of these places:

1 la place Grenette
2 le parc Paul-Mistral
3 l'Hôtel de Ville
4 l'église Saint-André
5 le stade municipal
6 les magasins du centre
7 la vieille ville

8	l'université
9	les instituts de géographie alpine et de géologie
10	la patinoire

1.2 Using *à* with distances

> **à une soixantaine de kilomètres d'ici**
> **à environ 100 mètres**

○ When expressing distances the patterns in English and French are different. Look at these examples:

L'Alpe-d'Huez est **à 627 kilomètres** de Paris.
L'Alpe-d'Huez is 627 kilometres from Paris.

La gare est à Grenoble, **à 60 kilomètres** de l'Alpe-d'Huez.
The station is in Grenoble, 60 kilometres from l'Alpe-d'Huez.

Chamrousse est **à une demi-heure** de Grenoble en voiture.
Chamrousse is half an hour by car from Grenoble.

La patinoire? C'est **à 100 mètres**, à côté de la piscine.
The ice rink? It's 100 metres away, next to the swimming pool.

○ The patterns are therefore as follows:

French: **à** + distance
(à 100 mètres)
English: distance + away
(100 metres away)

French: **à** + distance + **de** + place
(à 627 kilomètres de Paris)
English: distance + from + place
(627 kilometres from Paris)

B⟩⟩ Translate these sentences into French.

1 The station? It's 200 metres from the hotel.
2 The swimming pool? It's 50 metres from here, next to the ice rink.
3 Huez? It's a small village, about 4 kilometres from l'Alpe-d'Huez.
4 The hotel Le Christina? It's five minutes from here.

1.3 *De* + article + nouns

près du téléphérique
près de la piscine
près de l'église
près des magasins

○ Look at the following examples:

près **de** Grenoble
near Grenoble

près **de la** piscine
near the swimming pool

près **de l'**église
near the church

près **du** centre-ville
near the town centre

près **des** hôtels
near the hotels

○ Note that **de** changes form according to the article which follows. The rule is to use **de** in all cases except with **le** and **les** when **de + le** becomes **du** and **de + les** becomes **des**:

de + la → de la
de + l' → de l'
de + le → du
de + les → des

》 The guide in the tourist office at l'Alpe-d'Huez explains where places are by indicating what major buildings they are near. Use **C'est tout près de...** with each of these nouns.

1   la patinoire
2   l'héliport
3   la piscine
4   le syndicat d'initiative
5   les équipements sportifs

6   l'école de ski
7   le téléphérique
8   les remonte-pentes
9   l'arrêt de car
10 les magasins

1.4 *En* + present participle

en achetant un forfait-skieur
en prenant le car

○ Look at these examples showing how **en + present participle** are used to convey the idea of *doing something*:

En prenant le car de huit heures, on peut être là-haut à neuf heures.
By catching the eight o'clock coach, you can be up there by nine o'clock.

En arrivant là-bas assez tôt, on peut faire du ski toute la matinée et tout l'après-midi.
By arriving there fairly early, you can ski all morning and all afternoon.

○ The *present participle* is the form of the verb ending in **-ant** and is often used after **en**. It is derived from the nous form of the present tense – simply remove the **-ons** ending and add **-ant**. For example:

regarder → nous regardons → regard**ant**
faire → nous faisons → fais**ant**

(If you are not sure of the nous forms, see pages 37–8.)

○ There are only three exceptions:

être → étant
avoir → ayant
savoir → sachant

A›› Rephrase these sentences about getting the most out of a ski trip, by replacing the underlined sections with **en + present participle**.

1 <u>Si on fait</u> du ski tous les jours, on fait rapidement des progrès.
2 <u>Si on choisit</u> un bon moniteur, on est sûr d'apprendre plus rapidement.
3 <u>Si on se met</u> en forme avant, on est plus souple.
4 <u>Si on commence</u> à faire du ski à dix heures du matin, on peut faire six heures de ski par jour.
5 <u>Si on achète</u> un forfait-skieur, on paie beaucoup moins cher.
6 <u>Si on va</u> à 3000 mètres, on est sûr de trouver de la bonne neige.
7 <u>Si on partage</u> un chalet avec un groupe, on a l'occasion de se faire des amis.
8 <u>Si on prend</u> un repas rapide à midi, on peut faire du ski presque toute la journée.

○ **En + present participle** is also used to convey the idea of *on doing something* or *when you do something*:

> **En arrivant** au carrefour, vous devez tourner à gauche.
> *On reaching/When you reach the junction, you must turn left.*

B›› The hotel manager is telling M. Martens how to get to the coach station in Grenoble and finally to the ski-hire shop in l'Alpe-d'Huez. Rephrase what he says by replacing the underlined phrases with **en + present participle**.

1 <u>Quand vous sortirez</u> de l'hôtel, tournez à droite.
2 <u>Quand vous arriverez</u> au bout de l'avenue Alsace-Lorraine, vous verrez la gare à droite.
3 <u>Allez un peu plus loin et</u> vous vous trouverez devant la gare routière.
4 <u>Quand vous achèterez</u> votre billet, n'oubliez pas de demander un aller-retour.
5 <u>Quand vous descendrez</u> du car à l'Alpe-d'Huez, prenez la route du Signal.
6 <u>Quand vous verrez</u> le téléphérique, vous trouverez le magasin de M. Loup à droite.

○ **En + present participle** also conveys the idea of *while doing something*:

> Il a eu un accident **en descendant** de Chamrousse.
> *He had an accident while driving down from Chamrousse.*

C)) You're telling a fellow skier what happened to you at breakfast in the hotel before you set off. Rephrase your account by replacing the underlined phrases with en + present participle.

1 <u>Pendant que je prenais</u> mon petit déjeuner, j'ai parlé de ski à l'hôtelier.

2 Son fils s'est cassé le poignet <u>quand il faisait</u> du ski aux Deux-Alpes l'année dernière.

3 <u>Pendant que j'attendais</u> mon café, j'ai regardé un plan des pistes de l'Alpe-d'Huez.

4 <u>Comme je finissais</u> mon petit déjeuner, j'ai senti que le patron était de plus en plus inquiet.

5 <u>Comme je partais</u>, je l'ai entendu dire à sa femme: "Il va manquer le car, celui-là."

1.5 Prepositions + infinitive

pour aller

O **En + present participle** is similar to on doing, while doing, by doing (for example, en faisant du ski = *while skiing*) but it is important to note that very often the English present participle cannot be translated by the present participle in French. Look at these examples:

> Il est arrivé à l'Alpe-d'Huez **sans changer de car**.
> *He got to l'Alpe-d'Huez without changing buses.*

> **Avant de quitter** la gare routière, il a vérifié les horaires.
> *Before leaving the coach station, he checked the times.*

> **Il n'a pas eu de peine à descendre** une piste rouge et finalement il a réussi à descendre une piste noire sans incident.
> *He had no difficulty in going down a red run and finally he succeeded in skiing down a black run safely.*

> **Au lieu de retourner** à Grenoble à cinq heures, il a décidé de prendre le dernier car. **Il a arrêté de skier** à six heures.
> *Instead of returning to Grenoble at five, he decided to catch the last bus. He stopped skiing at six o'clock.*

○ Note that, with the exception of **en**, prepositions in French are followed by the *infinitive*, for example:

sans (*without*)

pour (*for/in order to*)

par – with verbs like **commencer par** and **finir par**

à – with verbs like **commencer à, réussir à**

de – with verbs like **arrêter de**, and phrases that contain **de** such as:

---

en train de faire (*in the middle of doing*)
sur le point de faire (*on the verge of doing*)
au lieu de faire (*instead of doing*)
afin de faire (*in order to do*)
avant de faire (*before doing*)

A⟩⟩ Use the correct form of the verb (present participle or infinitive) to complete this account of M. Martens' day at l'Alpe-d'Huez.

Sans (ÉCOUTER **1**) les conseils de l'hôtelier, il est sorti en (COURIR **2**) de l'hôtel. Au lieu d'(ALLER **3**) à la gare routière, il a cherché l'arrêt le plus proche dans l'espoir de (PRENDRE **4**) le car sans (DEVOIR **5**) aller jusqu'à la gare routière. Il a réussi à (TROUVER **6**) le bon arrêt. En (VOIR **7**) le car, il a levé le bras mais le car est passé sans même (RALENTIR **8**). Heureusement, un deuxième car est arrivé et il a fini par y (TROUVER **9**) une place. Il a réussi à (ARRIVER **10**) à l'Alpe-d'Huez en une heure et quart sans (CHANGER **11**) de car.

En (ARRIVER **12**), il a commencé par (CHERCHER **13**) la boutique de M. Loup afin d'y (LOUER **14**) des skis. Pour (S'ÉCHAUFFER **15**), il a commencé par (DESCENDRE **16**) plusieurs pistes bleues. Finalement, il a réussi à (DESCENDRE **17**) une piste noire sans difficulté.

B⟩⟩ Now translate the above passage into English.

1.6 Countries

> **en France**
> au Canada
> aux États-Unis
> **dans le sud-est de la France**
> l'avenir de la France
> la popularité de la France

○ Remember that *to* (a country) and *in* (a country) are always expressed in the same way in French.

With *feminine* names of countries use **en**:

> J'ai fait du ski **en** France, **en** Autriche et **en** Suisse.
> *I've skied in France, in Austria and in Switzerland.*

> L'année dernière, je suis allé **en** Autriche.
> *Last year I went to Austria.*

Note that **en** is also used with masculine names of countries beginning with a vowel, for example

en Iran, en Irak, en Afghanistan:

With *masculine* names of countries use **au**:

> **Au** Canada, le ski de fond est très répandu.
> *In Canada cross-country skiing is very popular.*

> J'espère aller **au** Canada l'hiver prochain.
> *I'm hoping to go to Canada next winter.*

With plural names of countries use **aux**:

> **Aux** États-Unis, le ski est un sport extrêmement à la mode.
> *In the United States skiing is a very popular sport.*

> Beaucoup de skieurs sont allés **aux** États-Unis cette année pour profiter de la neige abondante.
> *Many skiers went to the States this year to take advantage of the heavy snowfall.*

○ The rules for *from* (a country) follow a similar pattern with **de**:

Elle vient **de** France.
She comes from France.

Ils viennent **du** Canada.
They come from Canada.

Il vient **des** États-Unis.
He comes from the States.

A⟩⟩ Complete the text below, using **en, au, aux,** as appropriate. You will need to know the genders of these countries and continents:

masculine: le Portugal, le Canada, le Mexique, le Brésil, le Pérou
feminine: la Belgique, la France, l'Allemagne, l'Espagne, l'Amérique du Sud
plural: les Pays-Bas, les États-Unis

M. Martens habite à Anvers, _____ **(1)** Belgique mais il voyage beaucoup: _____ **(2)** Pays-Bas, _____ **(3)** France, _____ **(4)** Allemagne, _____ **(5)** Espagne, _____ **(6)** Portugal, même _____ **(7)** Canada et _____ **(8)** États-Unis. De temps en temps, il va _____ **(9)** Amérique du Sud, surtout _____ **(10)** Mexique, _____ **(11)** Brésil et _____ **(12)** Pérou.

B⟩⟩ Complete the text below, using **de, du** or **des**, as appropriate. You will need to know the genders of these countries, as well as those noted above:

masculine: le Chili
feminine: l'Argentine

Le fils de M. Martens vient de rentrer _____ **(1)** Amérique du Sud où il a passé six mois. Il a envoyé une seule lettre à ses parents, _____ **(2)** Chili pour leur demander de l'argent. Il a beaucoup voyagé: _____ **(3)** États-Unis au Mexique, _____ **(4)** Mexique au Brésil, _____ **(5)** Brésil en Argentine, _____ **(6)** Argentine au Chili, _____ **(7)** Chili aux États-Unis, et _____ **(8)** États-Unis en Belgique.

○ The rule with **de** also applies after the superlative:

> On dit que c'est la station **la plus ensoleillée de France**.
> *They say it's the sunniest ski resort in France.*

> C'est la station **la plus populaire du Canada**.
> *It's the most popular ski resort in Canada.*

> C'est **la meilleure station des États-Unis**.
> *It's the best ski resort in the States.*

L'Alpe-d'Huez est dans le sud-est de la France.

○ It is important to remember that the full form (for example **la France**) must be used except when translating *from a country* (**de France**) or when used after a superlative (**de France**). Look at these examples:

> ...dans le sud-est de **la France**.
> *...in the south-east of France.*

...l'avenir de **la France** comme centre mondial du ski.
...the future of France as a world-wide ski centre.

...la popularité **de la France** auprès des skieurs étrangers.
...the popularity of France with foreign skiers.

C)> Use either **France** or **la France** to complete these sentences about skiing in France.

En _____ (**1**), le ski est un sport très répandu. Le caractère montagneux de plusieurs régions de _____ (**2**) se prête facilement à de telles activités mais c'est surtout dans le sud-est de _____ (**3**) que les grandes stations se sont développées. C'est la meilleure région de _____ (**4**) pour les sports d'hiver. Les stations les plus célèbres de _____ (**5**) sont Val-d'Isère, Courchevel, Avoriaz et la Plagne. Si on veut aller en _____ (**6**) faire du ski, _____ (**7**) vous offre un choix énorme de stations; de l'Alpe-d'Huez, la station la plus ensoleillée de _____ (**8**) aux vieux villages savoyards qui rappellent toujours _____ (**9**) du dix-neuvième siècle. Beaucoup de skieurs étrangers vont en _____ (**10**) à Noël et à Pâques.

○ Note that English and French patterns are similar when referring to countries and the points of the compass. Look at these examples:

L'Alpe-d'Huez est **dans le sud-est** de la France.
L'Alpe-d'Huez is in the south-east of France.

L'Alpe-d'Huez est **au sud-est de** Grenoble.
L'Alpe-d'Huez is to the south-east of Grenoble.

D)> Translate these sentences into French.

1 Dunkirk is in the north of France.
2 Dunkirk is to the east of Calais.
3 La Chartreuse is to the north of Grenoble.
4 Versailles is to the west of Paris.
5 Bordeaux is in south-western France.

1.7 The pronoun *en*

> Je fais du ski de temps en temps. → **J'en fais de temps en temps.**
> Il y a deux ou trois cars par jour. → **Il y en a deux ou trois par jour.**

○ The pronoun **en** can mean *of it, of them, some,* or *any*. Look at these examples and note how **en** is used to replace **du, de la, de l', des** or **de** as well as the noun:

> – Tu as fait **du** ski?
> – *Have you done any skiing?*
> – J'**en** ai fait l'année dernière, et je vais aussi **en** faire cet hiver.
> – *I did some last year, and I'm going to do some this winter too.*
>
> – Tu fais beaucoup **de sport**?
> – *Do you do much sport?*
> – Pas maintenant. J'**en** faisais beaucoup quand j'étais au collège.
> – *Not now. I used to do a lot of it when I was at school.*
>
> – Tu as assez **d'argent** pour le déjeuner?
> – *Do you have enough money for lunch?*
> – Non, je n'**en** ai pas. J'ai laissé mon portefeuille au chalet.
> – *No, I don't have any. I left my wallet in the chalet.*

○ Note also how **en** can be used with a number.

> – Il y a deux pistes noires à l'Alpe-d'Huez?
> – *Are there two black runs at l'Alpe-d'Huez?*
> – Non, il y **en** a quatre.
> – *No, there are four (of them).*
>
> – Il y a des cars toute la journée?
> – *Are there coaches all day?*
> – Non, il y **en** a trois le matin et trois le soir.
> – *No, there are three (of them) in the morning and three in the evening.*

○ Note that the idea *of them* must be expressed in French. Il y a trois le matin et trois le soir without **en** would be incorrect.

>> The hotel manager shows great interest in M. Martens' experience of skiing and in how he's going to cope at l'Alpe-d'Huez. Add the necessary pronoun **en** in M. Martens' answers.

1   – Il y a des pistes artificielles en Belgique?
    – Oui, il y a trois ou quatre.
2   – Vous avez déjà fait du ski à l'étranger?
    – Oui, j'ai fait en Suisse et en Autriche.
3   – Les Belges aiment faire du ski?
    – Il y a qui adorent le ski.
4   – Vous avez des skis?
    – Non, je n'ai pas. Je vais louer à l'Alpe-d'Huez.
5   – Vous aurez besoin de crème solaire?
    – Je vais acheter là-haut.
6   – Vous voulez emprunter une carte de la région?
    – Non merci, j'ai une dans ma chambre.

Vous voulez emprunter une carte de la région?

1.8 *En* and *dans* in expressions of time

> On y arrive en 45 minutes.
> Le car part dans trois quarts d'heure.

○ Look at these examples showing how **en** and **dans** can both mean *in*:

> Il a appris à faire du ski **en** trois jours.
> *He learned to ski in three days.*
>
> Vous y arriverez **en** une heure et demie.
> *You will get there in an hour and a half.*
>
> Le car partira **dans** 10 minutes.
> *The coach will leave in 10 minutes.*
>
> Le télésiège fermera **dans** un quart d'heure.
> *The ski lift will close in a quarter of an hour.*

En is used to convey the idea of 'time taken to do something'.
Dans is used to convey the idea of 'in 10 minutes from now' or 'in a quarter of an hour's time'.

》 Use **en** or **dans** as appropriate to complete these snatches of conversation overheard at the ski resort.

1 J'ai fait beaucoup de progrès _____ trois jours.
2 La station va fermer _____ huit jours.
3 En montagne, le temps peut changer complètement _____ quelques heures.
4 Vous pourrez essayer une piste rouge _____ un jour ou deux.
5 Elle a descendu cette piste _____ trois minutes.
6 _____ deux ou trois jours la station va être presque déserte.
7 Les coureurs du Tour de France montent à l'Alpe-d'Huez _____ 45 minutes.
8 Il a été transporté à l'hôpital _____ une demi-heure.

1.9 Numbers

cent francs
mille francs
un million de francs
une soixantaine de kilomètres
plus de 20 nouvelles stations de ski

○ You probably already know that **une douzaine** means *a dozen* and that **une quinzaine de jours** means *a fortnight* (*about 15 days*). The suffix **-aine** can be added to most numbers to convey the idea of *about*. Look at these examples:

une vingtaine	*about 20*
une trentaine	*about 30*
une quarantaine	*about 40*
une centaine	*about 100*

Note that **un millier** is *about a thousand*.

○ All these words, as well as words like **un million** (*a million*) and **un milliard** (*a thousand million*) are nouns and must be followed by **de**:

une dizaine **d'**années	*about 10 years*
une centaine **de** personnes	*about 100 people*
un million **de** francs	*a million francs*

○ On the other hand, **cent** and **mille** are numbers and don't need **de**:

cent francs	*100 francs*
trois mille spectateurs	*3000 spectators*

○ Note how to say *hundreds of, thousands of*:

des centaines de policiers	*hundreds of policemen*
des milliers de manifestants	*thousands of demonstrators*

○ Remember that *more than* and *less than* with numbers is **plus de** and **moins de** (rather than **plus que** and **moins que**):

Il y a **plus de 20** grandes stations de ski dans cette région.
There are more than 20 major ski resorts in this area.

Les remonte-pentes étaient **à moins de 100** mètres de l'hôtel.
The ski lifts were less than 100 metres from the hotel.

>> Complete this text about French ski resorts, by adding **de, d', des** or nothing.

On compte plus _____ (1) cent _____ (2) stations de ski dans les Alpes françaises. Autour de Grenoble il y a une dizaine _____ (3) stations où l'hiver _____ (4) milliers _____ (5) Français font du ski tous les week-ends. Une vingtaine _____ (6) stations françaises ont une renommée internationale et attirent _____ (7) milliers _____ (8) skieurs étrangers tous les ans. Ils y dépensent _____ (9) millions _____ (10) francs puisque chacun y dépense au moins deux mille _____ (11) francs par semaine. Le tourisme français en bénéficie beaucoup, d'autant plus que moins _____ (12) dix pour cent des Français partent faire du ski à l'étranger.

2 Comparing the present and the past

A retired farm-worker, M. Ducellier, describes how the influx of commuters has changed life in Verneuil-sur-Seine.

…La vie a beaucoup changé depuis la guerre – et pas pour le mieux. Naturellement, **le travail était** très dur parce que	2.3
presque **tous les villageois travaillaient** la terre. **On**	2.3
commençait très tôt **le matin** et souvent **on ne rentrait pas**	2.3 / 2.5
pour déjeuner. À midi, **on mangeait** dans les champs. **Le**	2.3
soir, on était vraiment fatigué. Alors **on ne sortait pas**	2.3
beaucoup. **Le samedi** soir, **on allait** au bal de temps en	2.5 / 2.3
temps. **Le dimanche, on mettait** ses plus beaux vêtements	2.5 / 2.3
pour aller à l'église. Après, **c'était** le café. Mais **le soir,**	2.3 / 2.5

La vie a beaucoup changé!

généralement, **on restait** en famille: **on parlait** des incidents   2.3
de la journée, **on échangeait** des impressions et des   2.3
histoires. **Tout le monde se connaissait** et **on avait** le temps   2.8 / 2.3
de bavarder et d'être sociable.

Je ne crois pas que la vie d'aujourd'hui soit **aussi agréable**   2.1 / 2.6
qu'autrefois. Le village est devenu une petite ville. **Ce ne**   2.1
sont plus les mêmes familles qu'autrefois. **Beaucoup**   2.7
d'étrangers viennent s'installer ici. **Ils font** construire des   2.1
maisons un peu partout et **ils détruisent** peu à peu la   2.1
campagne… Tous les jours, **ils partent** travailler à Paris. **Ils**
prennent le même train. Et **le week-end, ils ne font pas**   2.5 / 2.1
grand-chose: ils veulent simplement se reposer.   2.1
Naturellement, **ils doivent** aller faire les courses au
supermarché. **Ils vont** partout en voiture et **ils conduisent**   2.1
trop vite. Même **s'ils vous voient** en ville, **ils ne vous disent**   2.1
pas bonjour. Le reste du week-end, **ils s'enferment** dans   2.1
leurs petits pavillons et **on ne les voit plus. Ils ne savent**   2.1 / 2.4
pas s'adapter à la vie rurale. **On est plus riche que par le**   2.6
passé mais moi, je trouve qu'**on est moins heureux**. Comme   2.6
la vie a changé!

2.1 The present tense

ils font	ils partent
ils vont	ils conduisent
ils veulent	ils savent
ils doivent	ils disent
ils prennent	

O The present tense is used to talk about:
  i.   what is going on at the moment
  ii. what people habitually do or what is generally true.

> – Que **fait** Julien?
> – *What's Julian doing?*

> – Il **fait** ses devoirs dans sa chambre.
> – *He's doing his homework in his room.*

De plus en plus de Français **passent** leurs vacances à l'étranger.
More and more French people spend (or are spending) their holidays abroad.

O Remember that the two English versions (*spend/are spending*) are expressed by one form only in French: **ils passent**.

O Never use the verb **être** to translate '*they are spending*', '*they are living*'; you just need the present tense of the correct verb: **ils passent, ils habitent**.

O Here are the three major conjugations, showing the forms of the present tense for regular verbs:

– **er** verbs (like regard**er**)	– **ir** verbs (like fin**ir**)	– **re** verbs (like vend**re**)
je regard**e**	je fin**is**	je vend**s**
tu regard**es**	tu fin**is**	tu vend**s**
il/elle/on regard**e**	il/elle/on fin**it**	il/elle/on vend
nous regard**ons**	nous fin**issons**	nous vend**ons**
vous regard**ez**	vous fin**issez**	vous vend**ez**
ils/elles regard**ent**	ils/elles fin**issent**	ils/elles vend**ent**

○ There are a number of **-er** verbs which have small spelling changes in the present tense. One of them is **espérer**:

j'esp**è**re	il/elle esp**è**re	vous esp**é**rez
tu esp**è**res	nous esp**é**rons	ils/elles esp**è**rent

The rule is that the **é** used in the infinitive spelling (espérer) is used when the ending is pronounced (espérer, nous espérons, vous espérez) and that **è** is used when the ending is silent (j'espère, il/elle espère, tu espères, ils/elles espèrent).

Other important verbs like **espérer** are:

préférer	protéger	suggérer
répéter	refléter	céder
posséder	considérer	s'inquiéter
exagérer	sécher	

○ Verbs like **acheter** follow a slightly different pattern:

j'ach**è**te	nous ach**e**tons
tu ach**è**tes	vous ach**e**tez
il/elle/on ach**è**te	ils/elles ach**è**tent

The infinitive spelling (acheter) is used if the ending is pronounced (nous achetons, vous achetez) and **è** is used when the ending is silent (j'achète, tu achètes, il/elle achète, ils/elles achètent).

Other important verbs which follow this pattern are:

mener	soulever
amener	crever
emmener	peser
(se) promener	geler
(se) lever	

○ Other verbs have the infinitive spelling if the ending is sounded but double the consonant if there is a silent ending. Look at **s'appeler** as an example:

je m'appe**ll**e	nous nous appe**l**ons
tu t'appe**ll**es	vous vous appe**l**ez
il/elle/on s'appe**ll**e	ils/elles s'appe**ll**ent

Other verbs which follow this pattern are:

se rappeler	rejeter
renouveler	projeter
jeter	

29

○ Verbs ending in **-yer** only keep the **y** in the nous and vous forms. Look at **payer** as an example:

je pa**i**e	nous pa**y**ons
tu pa**i**es	vous pa**y**ez
il/elle/on pa**i**e	ils/elles pa**i**ent

Other important verbs which follow this pattern are:

employer	appuyer
essayer	s'ennuyer
nettoyer	

○ Many important verbs are irregular. A useful point to remember is that the **je** and **tu** forms of all irregular verbs end in **-s** (except for j'**ai**, je **veux**, tu **veux**, je **peux**, tu **peux**, j'**offre** and verbs like it listed on page 33). Similarly, **il/elle** forms of irregular verbs end in **-t** (except for il/elle **va**, il/elle **a**, il/elle **prend**).

○ The following table shows the most common irregular verbs:

Infinitive	Present tense		Similar verbs
aller to go	je vais	nous allons	
	tu vas	vous allez	
	il/elle/on va	ils/elles vont	
avoir to have	j'ai	nous avons	
	tu as	vous avez	
	il/elle/on a	ils/elles ont	
battre to beat	je bats	nous battons	combattre, débattre
	tu bats	vous battez	
	il/elle/on bat	ils/elles battent	
boire drink	je bois	nous buvons	
	tu bois	vous buvez	
	il/elle/on boit	ils/elles boivent	

Infinitive	Present tense		Similar verbs
conduire to drive	je conduis tu conduis il/elle/on conduit	nous conduisons vous conduisez ils/elles conduisent	verbs ending in -uire: produire, introduire, construire, détruire, traduire, réduire
connaître to know	je connais tu connais il/elle/on connaît	nous connaissons vous connaissez ils/elles connaissent	reconnaître, (ap)paraître, disparaître
courir to run	je cours tu cours il/elle/on court	nous courons vous courez ils/elles courent	
craindre to fear	je crains tu crains il/elle/on craint	nous craignons vous craignez ils/elles craignent	verbs ending in -aindre, -eindre, -oindre: se plaindre, contraindre, peindre, atteindre, éteindre, restreindre, (re)joindre
croire to believe	je crois tu crois il/elle/on croit	nous croyons vous croyez ils/elles croient	
devoir to have to	je dois tu dois il/elle/on doit	nous devons vous devez ils/elles doivent	recevoir, apercevoir

Infinitive	Present tense		Similar verbs
dire			
to say	je dis	nous disons	prédire, interdire,
	tu dis	vous dites	contredire
	il/elle/on dit	ils/elles disent	
écrire			
to write	j'écris	nous écrivons	décrire
	tu écris	vous écrivez	
	il/elle/on écrit	ils/elles écrivent	
être			
to be	je suis	nous sommes	
	tu es	vous êtes	
	il/elle/on est	ils/elles sont	
faire			
to do,	je fais	nous faisons	défaire, satisfaire
to make	tu fais	vous faites	
	il/elle/on fait	ils/elles font	
lire			
to read	je lis	nous lisons	élire
	tu lis	vous lisez	
	il/elle/on lit	ils/elles lisent	
mettre			
to put	je mets	nous mettons	permettre, promettre,
	tu mets	vous mettez	admettre, commettre
	il/elle/on met	ils/elles mettent	
mourir			
to die	je meurs	nous mourons	
	tu meurs	vous mourez	
	il/elle/on meurt	ils/elles meurent	

Infinitive	Present tense		Similar verbs
offrir to offer	j'offre tu offres il/elle/on offre	nous offrons vous offrez ils/elles offrent	ouvrir, découvrir, couvrir, souffrir
partir to leave	je pars tu pars il/elle/on part	nous partons vous partez ils/elles partent	sortir, dormir, servir, sentir, mentir
pouvoir to be able to	je peux tu peux il/elle/on peut	nous pouvons vous pouvez ils/elles peuvent	
prendre to take	je prends tu prends il/elle/on prend	nous prenons vous prenez ils/elles prennent	apprendre, comprendre, entreprendre
recevoir to receive	je reçois tu reçois il/elle/on reçoit	nous recevons vous recevez ils/elles reçoivent	apercevoir
rire to laugh	je ris tu ris il/elle/on rit	nous rions vous riez ils/elles rient	sourire
savoir to know	je sais tu sais il/elle/on sait	nous savons vous savez ils/elles savent	

Infinitive	Present tense		Similar verbs
suivre to follow	je suis tu suis il/elle/on suit	nous suivons vous suivez ils/elles suivent	poursuivre
venir to come	je viens tu viens il/elle/on vient	nous venons vous venez ils/elles viennent	revenir, devenir, convenir, tenir, contenir, appartenir, maintenir, etc
vivre to live	je vis tu vis il/elle/on vit	nous vivons vous vivez ils/elles vivent	survivre
voir to see	je vois tu vois il/elle/on voit	nous voyons vous voyez ils/elles voient	revoir, prévoir, entrevoir, etc.
vouloir to want	je veux tu veux il/elle/on veut	nous voulons vous voulez ils/elles veulent	

Je dors de temps en temps.

A》 Learn the **je** and **vous** forms of the irregular verbs listed above. Then, without consulting the list, complete this dialogue by putting the verb in brackets into the present tense.

A reporter from the local newspaper is interviewing older people to see how they are adapting to the changes in Verneuil.

– Alors, M. Ducellier, vous (SAVOIR **1**) conduire?
– Moi? Mais non, je ne (SAVOIR **2**) pas conduire. Mais je (ALLER **3**) au café de temps en temps à vélo!
– Que (FAIRE **4**)-vous au café?
– Je (LIRE **5**) le journal, je (FAIRE **6**) une partie de cartes avec un groupe d'amis que je (CONNAÎTRE **7**) depuis longtemps. Je leur (OFFRIR **8**) un verre de temps en temps…
– Que (BOIRE **9**)- vous généralement?
– Moi? Je (BOIRE **10**) du vin rouge et quelquefois du cognac.
– Et vous (VOIR **11**) souvent vos amis?
– Je les (VOIR **12**) deux ou trois fois par semaine.
Je ne (SORTIR **13**) pas beaucoup maintenant. Je ne (POUVOIR **14**) pas toujours faire l'effort nécessaire.
– Mais vous (VIVRE **15**) seul?
– Oui, je (VIVRE **16**) seul depuis la mort de ma femme.
Je (DEVOIR **17**) m'occuper un peu de la maison. En fait, je ne (VOULOIR **18**) pas sortir plus souvent. J'(AVOIR **19**) la télévision. Je la (METTRE **20**) vers six heures.
J'(APPRENDRE **21**) toutes sortes de choses intéressantes – et je (DORMIR **22**) de temps en temps! Je (CROIRE **23**) que je (VIVRE **24**) bien!

○   Note in particular the **ils/elles** forms.

   i.   regular verbs follow these patterns:

         -er verbs, for example:
         pass**er** *to spend* → ils/elles pass**ent**

         -ir verbs, for example:
         fin**ir** *to finish* → ils/elles fin**issent**

         -re verbs, for example:
         vend**re** */to sell* → ils/elles vend**ent**

ii. note these important irregular verbs:

aller	*to go*	ils/elles vont
avoir	*to have*	ils/elles ont
boire	*to drink*	ils/elles boivent
conduire	*to drive*	ils/elles conduisent
connaître	*to know*	ils/elles connaissent
courir	*to run*	ils/elles courent
craindre	*to fear*	ils/elles craignent
croire	*to believe*	ils/elles croient
devoir	*to have to*	ils/elles doivent
dire	*to say*	ils/elles disent
écrire	*to write*	ils/elles écrivent
être	*to be*	ils/elles sont
faire	*to do/make*	ils/elles font
lire	*to read*	ils/elles lisent
mettre	*to put*	ils/elles mettent
mourir	*to die*	ils/elles meurent
offrir	*to offer*	ils/elles offrent
partir	*to leave*	ils/elles partent
pouvoir	*to be able to*	ils/elles peuvent
prendre	*to take*	ils/elles prennent
recevoir	*to receive*	ils/elles reçoivent
savoir	*to know*	ils/elles savent
sortir	*to go out*	ils/elles sortent
venir	*to come*	ils/elles viennent
voir	*to see*	ils/elles voient
vouloir	*to want to*	ils/elles veulent

B⟩⟩ Put the verbs in brackets into the present tense to complete the description of what life is like for commuters in Verneuil.

Beaucoup de banlieusards ne (FAIRE **1**) rien le week-end. Ils (VOULOIR **2**) simplement se reposer. Ils ne (PRENDRE **3**) pas la peine de communiquer avec leurs voisins: le soir ils n'(AVOIR **4**) pas le temps de parler aux voisins et le week-ends ils (ÊTRE **5**) trop fatigués pour établir le contact. Ils ne (POUVOIR **6**) pas faire l'effort nécessaire pour se faire des amis. Souvent les gens ne (CONNAÎTRE **7**) pas leurs voisins. Ils ne (VOIR **8**) pas souvent leurs voisins, parce qu'ils (ALLER **9**) partout en voiture. Ils (CONDUIRE **10**) presque tous trop vite. Ils (VENIR **11**) à la campagne pour éviter la promiscuité des grands ensembles. Ils (DEVOIR **12**) essayer de s'adapter à la vie rurale mais beaucoup d'entre eux ne (SAVOIR **13**) pas jardiner, par exemple.

○ The nous forms of the present tense are especially important as they also form the basis of the imperfect tense.

   i. regular verbs follow these patterns:

     -er verbs, for example:
     pass**er** *to spend* → nous pass**ons**

     -ir verbs, for example:
     fin**ir** *to finish* → nous fin**issons**

     -re verbs, for example:
     attend**re** *to wait* → nous attend**ons**

     -ger verbs, for example:
     mang**er** *to eat* → nous mang**eons**

     -cer verbs, for example:
     commenc**er** *to start* → nous commen**çons**

   ii. note these important irregular verbs:

avoir	*to have*	→ nous avons
boire	*to drink*	→ nous buvons
conduire	*to drive*	→ nous conduisons
connaître	*to know*	→ nous connaissons
courir	*to run*	→ nous courons
craindre	*to fear*	→ nous craignons
croire	*to believe*	→ nous croyons
devoir	*to have to*	→ nous devons

Ils conduisent presque tous trop vite!

dire	*to say*	→ nous disons
dormir	*to sleep*	→ nous dormons
écrire	*to write*	→ nous écrivons
être	*to be*	→ nous sommes
faire	*to do/make*	→ nous faisons
lire	*to read*	→ nous lisons
offrir	*to offer*	→ nous offrons
partir	*to leave*	→ nous partons
pouvoir	*to be able to*	→ nous pouvons
prendre	*to take*	→ nous prenons
recevoir	*to receive*	→ nous recevons
savoir	*to know*	→ nous savons
sortir	*to go out*	→ nous sortons
venir	*to come*	→ nous venons
vouloir	*to want to*	→ nous voulons

◖❯ Put the verb in brackets into the present tense to complete what the newcomers have to say about their life in the suburbs.

Nous (AIMER **1**) beaucoup notre petite ville. Nous (AVOIR **2**) un petit pavillon. Nous ne (SORTIR **3**) pas beaucoup le week-end – nous (FAIRE **4**) du jardinage ou du bricolage. Nous (LIRE **5**) aussi. Quelquefois, l'après-midi, nous (DORMIR **6**) un peu! Avant le dîner, nous (PRENDRE **7**) l'apéritif dans le jardin. S'il fait assez chaud, nous (MANGER **8**) aussi dans le jardin. Nous ne (CONNAÎTRE **9**) pas très bien nos voisins, mais nous (COMMENCER **10**) à parler avec eux. Nous leur (DIRE **11**) bonjour aussi souvent que possible.

2.2   The present tense of reflexive verbs

Check carefully the forms of the reflexive verbs in this conversation between M. Ducellier and his daughter:

– **Tu te réveilles** de bonne heure?
– Oui, **je me réveille** vers 4 heures du matin. Nous autres vieux, **on se réveille** très tôt.
– Et **vous vous endormez** dans la journée, hein?
– Oui, **nous nous endormons** très facilement à notre âge. Les vieux, **ils se fatiguent** très vite, tu sais…

D》 Put the verb in brackets into the present tense.

Mon ami, Paul, et moi (SE RETROUVER) presque tous les jours.
Nous (SE PROMENER) un peu jusqu'à la place. Nous
(S'INSTALLER) au café. Le patron (S'OCCUPER) gentiment de
nous. Nous (SE RACONTER) des histoires du passé... "Tu (SE
RAPPELER) le jour où...?" "Tu (SE SOUVENIR) du soir où...?" On
(SE DISPUTER) quelquefois sur ce qui s'est vraiment passé mais en
général on (S'ENTENDRE) bien. Les autres ne (S'INTÉRESSER) pas
à nos histoires: ils (S'AMUSER) à regarder le foot à la télé...
Quelquefois ils (SE MOQUER) de nous: "Vous ne (S'ENNUYER) pas
avec toutes ces vieilles histoires?" A vrai dire, on ne (S'ENNUYER)
jamais.

2.3 The imperfect tense

c'était	on finissait
on avait	on vivait
il y avait	**on mangeait**
on travaillait	**on commençait**

○ The imperfect tense is used mainly to convey the idea of what was
generally true in the past, what people used to do, what their lives
were like.

○ There is only one set of endings to learn for the imperfect tense.
Here are the endings used with the verb être:

j'ét**ais**	*I was/used to be*
tu ét**ais**	*you were/used to be*
il/elle/on ét**ait**	*he/she/one was/used to be*
nous ét**ions**	*we were/used to be*
vous ét**iez**	*you were/used to be*
ils/elles ét**aient**	*they were/used to be*

○ Watch out especially for the three different spellings of the same sound:

> j'ét**ais**
> il/elle ét**ait**
> ils/elles ét**aient**

○ In the imperfect tense, the stem of all verbs (except être) is derived from the nous form of the ***present tense*** (see pages 37–8). Here are some examples – the **-ons** ending is removed from the **nous** form of the present tense, then the appropriate imperfect ending is added:

prendre	→ nous **pre**nons	→ je **pren**ais
boire	→ nous **bu**vons	→ il **buv**ait
manger	→ nous **mange**ons	→ elle **mange**ait
commencer	→ nous **commenç**ons	→ on **commenç**ait

A⟩⟩ Add the correct imperfect endings to the following verbs. The correct stem has already been supplied for you.

1 (FAIRE) Il fais___
2 (CONDUIRE) Nous conduis___
3 (PRENDRE) Ils pren___
4 (FINIR) Je finiss___
5 (JOUER) Nous jou___
6 (LIRE) Elle lis___
7 (TRAVAILLER) Elles travaill___
8 (MANGER) Je mange___

B⟩⟩ Complete M. Ducellier's account of what life was like when Verneuil was still a farming community and when he used to work on the land. Put the verbs in brackets into the imperfect tense. Remember to check the stem carefully before you add the endings.

Je (TRAVAILLER **1**) très dur – je (COMMENCER **2**) à six heures du matin et je (FINIR **3**) à cinq heures du soir. À midi, j'(AVOIR **4**) une demi-heure de repos. D'habitude, je (MANGER **5**) dans les champs. Le soir, j'(ÊTRE **6**) très fatigué, et donc je ne (SORTIR **7**) pas très souvent. Quelquefois, je (LIRE **8**) un peu et de temps en temps je (PRENDRE **9**) un verre au café. Le dimanche, je ne (FAIRE **10**) pas grand-chose. Je (METTRE **11**) mon costume et j'(ALLER **12**) à l'église. Après la messe, je (BOIRE **13**) un apéritif. Je (CONNAÎTRE **14**) tout le monde et tout le monde me (DIRE **15**) bonjour.

2.4 *Savoir* or *pouvoir*?

> **ils ne savent pas**

○ The verbs **savoir** and **pouvoir** can both be used to translate *can* in English. Look at this example.

Je **sais** nager, mais je ne **peux** pas nager en ce moment. J'ai un rhume.

Use **savoir** to translate *'to know how to do something'* and **pouvoir** to translate *'to be able to do something because circumstances allow'*.

》 Use the correct form of **pouvoir** or **savoir**, as appropriate, to complete the gaps in this article about the way the new inhabitants of Verneuil are adapting to country life. (See pages 33–4 for the forms of savoir and pouvoir.)

Les banlieusards de Verneuil qui habitent à 30 kilomètres de Paris ne _____ **(1)** pas facilement y aller le week-end. C'est trop loin. Mais on dit que beaucoup d'entre eux ne _____ **(2)** pas non plus s'adapter à la vie rurale. Ils _____ **(3)** bricoler un peu et ils _____ **(4)** utiliser la tronçonneuse pour couper les arbres qu'ils trouvent sur leur terrain! En général, ils ne _____ **(5)** pas jardiner. Ils ont de l'argent et ils _____ **(6)** donc acheter des plantes mais ils ne _____ **(7)** pas toujours s'en occuper. Alors qu'est-ce qu'ils _____ **(8)** faire pour profiter de leur nouvel environnement? Ils _____ **(9)** faire du footing et ils _____ **(10)** aller à la pêche. S'ils ne _____ **(11)** pas faire de la voile, ils _____ **(12)** apprendre à en faire à la base de loisirs. S'ils _____ **(13)** jouer au bridge, ils _____ **(14)** s'inscrire au club local. En participant à toutes ces activités, ils _____ **(15)** s'intégrer assez facilement à la vie sociale de leur nouvelle ville.

2.5 How to translate *in the morning, at the weekend, on Sundays*

> **le matin**
> **le soir**
> **le samedi**
> **le dimanche**
> **le week-end**

○ Phrases like *in the morning, in the evening, at the weekend, on Sundays* are usually expressed in French quite simply by **le matin, le soir, le week-end, le dimanche**. Other translations are of course possible, for example: **tous les matins, chaque soir, les dimanches,** but these are less commonly used.

Similarly, *in the summer* and *in the winter* can be expressed by **l'été** and **l'hiver** (as well as **en été** and **en hiver**).

○ If a specific time is mentioned, then a different construction is used. Look at these examples:

Il commençait le travail à six heures **du matin**.
He used to begin work at six o'clock in the morning.

Il finissait le travail à cinq heures **de l'après-midi**.
He finished work at five o'clock in the afternoon.

>> Translate the phrases in brackets to complete this account of what M. Ducellier's daily routine was like when he worked on the land.

(IN THE MORNING 1), M. Ducellier se levait très tôt. (IN THE SUMMER 2), il se levait à cinq heures (IN THE MORNING 3) et il travaillait jusqu'à neuf heures (IN THE EVENING 4). (IN THE WINTER 5), il finissait le travail vers cinq heures (IN THE EVENING 6). (IN THE EVENINGS 7), il sortait très peu. (AT THE WEEKEND 8) ou plutôt (ON SUNDAYS 9), parce qu'il travaillait (ON SATURDAYS 10), il sortait un peu. (ON SATURDAY EVENINGS 11), il allait quelquefois au bal et (ON SUNDAY MORNINGS 12), il allait au café et il y restait jusqu'à trois heures (IN THE AFTERNOON 13).

2.6 The comparative form of adjectives

plus riche que
moins heureux que
aussi agréable que

○ When making comparisons in French, **plus... que** is used to translate *more... than* and **moins... que** to translate *less... than*.

Les rues sont **plus encombrées que** dans les années 50.
The streets are more congested than in the fifties.

La vie est beaucoup **moins tranquille que** par le passé.
Life is much less relaxed than in the past.

A⟩⟩ M. Ducellier is not so keen on the changes that have taken place during his lifetime. Complete the sentences below using **plus** or **moins** to reflect his attitude.

1. La vie était ___ dure quand j'étais jeune parce qu'on était ___ pauvre.
2. Autrefois les rues étaient ___ encombrées qu'aujourd'hui. Le village était beaucoup ___ calme.
3. On était ___ pressé: on avait le temps de se parler longuement.
4. A cette époque les gens étaient ___ sociables et décontractés: ils étaient ___ fatigués et ___ tendus.
5. Le marché du samedi était ___ animé que maintenant.

○ If you want to convey the idea of *as… as*, use **aussi que**. Look at these examples:

La Seine est **aussi belle que** par le passé.
The Seine is as beautiful as it was in the past.

Les paysages sont **aussi jolis que** par le passé.
The scenery is as pretty as it was in the past.

○ Note that **aussi… que** can be shortened to **si… que** after a negative:

Le village n'est pas **si** tranquille **qu'**autrefois.
The village is not as quiet as it once was.

La forêt n'est pas **si** grande **qu'**il y a 30 ans.
The forest is not as big as it was 30 years ago.

B⟩⟩ Look at these two versions of the same idea.

i. La vie n'est **pas si agréable que** par le passé.
Life is not as pleasant as…

ii La vie est **moins agréable que** par le passé.
Life is less pleasant than…

⟩⟩ The following sentences follow the pattern in the second version. Rephrase them so that they are similar to the first version.

1 Le bal du samedi soir est moins fréquenté qu'autrefois.
2 Le travail à la ferme est moins dur qu'autrefois.
3 Le village est moins animé le dimanche.
4 Les sentiments de solidarité sont moins forts que par le passé.
5 Les jardins sont moins grands qu'autrefois.

2.7 *Le même... que* (the same... as)

les mêmes familles qu'autrefois

○ There are three forms of *the same as* in French, depending on whether the noun is masculine, feminine or plural. Look at these examples:

> À cette époque-là, on avait **le même** mode de vie **que** ses voisins.
> *In those days you led the same kind of life as the neighbours.*

> Le dimanche, on allait à **la même** église **que** les autres.
> *On Sundays you went to the same church as the others.*

> On connaissait **les mêmes** familles **que** les autres.
> *You knew the same families as everyone else.*

>> When M. Ducellier was young, life was much the same for everybody. Complete what he says by translating the section in brackets into French. Use the following vocabulary:

| une école | le travail |
| une classe | les préoccupations |

1 J'allais à (THE SAME SCHOOL AS) les autres.
2 J'étais dans (THE SAME CLASS AS) tous les autres.
3 Nos parents faisaient (THE SAME WORK AS) leurs voisins.
4 Ils avaient (THE SAME CONCERNS AS) les autres.

Ils s'entendaient très bien.

2.8 How to translate *each other*

Tout le monde se connaissait

○ To convey the idea of *each other*, you often have to use a reflexive verb. With the third person plural (ils/elles forms) the reflexive pronoun used with the verb is **se**:

> Tous les villageois **se** connaissaient.
> *All the people in the village knew each other.*

> Ils **se** donnaient un coup de main lors des gros travaux.
> *They gave each other a hand at busy times of the year.*

○ Note that in English you can sometimes omit *each other*, but that in French you always need the reflexive pronoun as well as the verb:

> Ils **se** rencontraient au café.
> *They used to meet in the café.*

A》 The village community was close-knit and friendly. Complete this text by translating the sections in brackets into French. You will need to use the following verbs in the imperfect tense.

(se) retrouver	(se) dire bonjour	(se) serrer la main
(s') entendre	(s') entraider	(se) revoir
(se) parler	(se) réunir	

Autrefois les gens du village (MET **1**) plusieurs fois par jour. (THEY SAID HELLO AND SHOOK HANDS **2**). S'il y avait des problèmes, (THEY HELPED EACH OTHER OUT **3**). (THEY GOT ON **4**) très bien. Quand (THEY SAW EACH OTHER **5**) dans la rue, (THEY TALKED **6**) longuement, et le soir (THEY MET **7**) aussi souvent que possible.

B》 Now translate the whole passage into English.

3 Talking about past experiences and expressing opinions

Comme on a bien mangé!

Mme Dupuy describes the relaxing and satisfying camping holiday she and her family had on the Atlantic coast of France this summer.

Mme Barre:	**Vous avez passé de bonnes vacances** cet été?	3.1
Mme Dupuy:	Oui, **nous nous sommes tous très bien amusés**.	3.7
Mme Barre:	**Vous êtes allés** où?	3.7
Mme Dupuy:	**Nous sommes allés** sur la côte Atlantique, à une vingtaine de kilomètres des Sables-d'Olonne.	3.7
Mme Barre:	Je ne connais pas cette côte. C'est bien, là-bas?	
Mme Dupuy:	C'est formidable! Il y a **de très belles plages** sablonneuses, **des plages magnifiques**! Moi, je crois que c'est **la plus belle côte de France**.	3.1 3.1 3.2
Mme Barre:	Et il y a **de bons équipements**?	3.1

Mme Dupuy:	Il y a **tous les équipements dont on pourrait**	3.5 / 3.4
	avoir besoin. Il y a **énormément de choses** à	3.6
	faire. **Les enfants se sont baignés**, même si	3.7
	l'eau était plutôt froide, **ils ont fait** de la	3.7
	planche à voile, du cheval. Ils ont fait **toutes**	3.5
	sortes de choses.	
Mme Barre:	Vous étiez à l'hôtel?	
Mme Dupuy:	Non, **on a fait** du camping. Il y a **un certain**	3.7 / 3.6
	nombre de grands hôtels (mais il y a surtout	
	beaucoup de campings dont la réputation	3.6 / 3.4
	est excellente et qui ne sont pas trop chers).	3.4
Mme Barre:	Moi, je trouve que les campings sont si	
	bruyants et encombrés.	
Mme Dupuy:	Là-bas, **la plupart des campings** sont grands	3.6
	et **chaque** emplacement est entouré d'arbres	3.5
	ou de haies. **On m'a dit** que c'était **le**	3.7 / 3.2
	meilleur camping de la région. Le soir et la	3.9
	nuit, **tout était** très calme. **Tout le monde**,	3.5
	était très sympathique et c'est ça **que** j'aime	3.4
	avant tout. **Tout le monde se parle**. On se	3.5
	retrouve **tout le temps**, au terrain de jeux, à la	3.5
	laverie.	
Mme Barre:	Mais **vous avez dû** préparer **tous les repas**	3.7 / 3.5
	vous-même?	
Mme Dupuy:	Au contraire, **j'ai préparé très peu de** repas.	3.7 / 3.6
	Nous faisions un pique-nique à midi et **la**	3.9
	plupart du temps, nous allions tous au	3.6 / 3.9
	restaurant le soir. Là-bas, on trouve **les**	
	meilleurs fruits de mer de France. Comme	3.2
	on a bien mangé! Ce sont **les meilleures**	3.2 / 3.3
	vacances que j'aie jamais passées! Je **viens**	3.8
	de faire développer nos photos. Je vais vous	
	les montrer.	

3.1 *Des* or *de*?

> des plages magnifiques
> de belles plages
> de bonnes vacances

○ Look at these two examples from the dialogue:
   i.   Sur la côte Atlantique, il y a **des** plages magnifiques.
   ii. Sur la côte Atlantique, il y a **de** belles plages.

Whether you use **des** or **de** depends on the position of the adjective. In the first example the adjective **magnifiques** comes after the noun. In such cases, **des** is used. In the second example, the adjective **belles** comes before the noun. When this happens, **de** is used.

A)⟩ Use de or des to complete this list of what the Atlantic coast has to offer tourists.

1   ___ villages pittoresques
2   ___ plages sablonneuses
3   ___ petits ports de pêche
4   ___ beaux campings
5   ___ grands hôtels
6   ___ bons équipements

B)⟩ Rewrite this extract from a tourist brochure, by replacing the underlined adjectives with a suitable adjective from the box below. Remember that these adjectives come before the noun.

| grand | beau | petit | joli | nouveau | nombreux | bon | vieux |

1   Il y a des stations balnéaires <u>modernes</u> mais on trouve aussi des ports de pêche <u>pittoresques</u>.
2   Il y a des campings <u>énormes</u> où <u>beaucoup</u> d'Anglais passent leurs vacances parce qu'il y a des plages <u>magnifiques</u> tout le long de cette côte.
3   À la campagne, il y a des maisons <u>de taille très modeste</u> qu'on peut louer à la quinzaine ou au mois.
4   Il y a aussi des châteaux <u>anciens</u> qu'on peut visiter.
5   Dans cette région, on peut passer des vacances très <u>agréables</u>.

◖)) This extract from a travel brochure on where to stay and what to do on the Atlantic coast has mistakes in some of the underlined sections. Rewrite the extract, correcting anything that is wrong.

Sur cette côte, il y a <u>des grands campings</u> (**1**) où <u>de nombreuses familles françaises</u> (**2**) viennent passer leurs vacances. <u>Des autres estivants</u> (**3**) préfèrent les grandes stations où on trouve <u>des grands hôtels</u> (**4**) qui donnent sur la mer. Il y a des stations qui sont là depuis <u>de longues années</u> (**5**) et <u>des autres</u> (**6**) qui ont été construites depuis la guerre. On peut visiter <u>des jolis ports de pêche</u> (**7**) et de là on peut faire <u>des promenades en mer agréables.</u> (**8**) Tout autour des ports, il y a <u>des bons petits restaurants</u> (**9**) où on peut manger <u>des fruits de mer délicieux</u> (**10**).

3.2 The superlative

la plus belle côte de France
le village le plus pittoresque de la région
le meilleur camping de la région

○ Look at these two examples.

i. C'est **le plus grand camping** de la région.
It's the biggest campsite in the area.

ii. C'est **le camping le plus luxueux** de la région.
It's the best-equipped campsite in the area.

You can see that there are two versions of the superlative in French. The first version is used when the adjective comes **before** the noun. The most common of these adjectives are:

grand	petit	nouveau	vieux	beau	joli	jeune	gros	haut
bon	mauvais	excellent	long	court	autre	nombreux		

The second version is used when the adjective comes **after** the noun.

○ Note that **le moins**… can be used in the same way to translate *the least*… For example:

C'est le camping **le moins cher**.
It's the least expensive campsite.

Watch out for the adjustments you must make when feminine and plural nouns are involved.

C'est **la plus grande station balnéaire** de la région.
It's the largest seaside resort in the area.

C'est la station balnéaire **la plus importante** de la région.
It's the most important seaside resort in the area.

Ce sont **les stations les plus populaires** de la côte.
They are the most popular seaside resorts on the coast.

A》 Look at the five basic examples above. Then rephrase these sentences using a superlative in each case. Complete each sentence with... **de la région**.

1   C'est un très grand port de pêche.
2   C'est une station très chère.
3   C'est une église très ancienne.
4   C'est un très joli village.
5   C'est une station très moderne.
6   C'est une très belle plage.
7   Ce sont des hôtels très confortables.
8   Ce sont des campings très tranquilles.

O   Note that the superlative of bon is **meilleur** *(best)*. Look at these examples showing the different forms of *the best* in French:

C'est **le meilleur hôtel** de la ville.
C'est **la meilleure piscine** de la région.
Ce sont **les meilleurs campings** de la région.
Ce sont **les meilleures stations** de la région.

O   Note that after a superlative the English idea of *in the area, in the town* is expressed by **de** in French: **de la région, de la ville**. Similarly, *in France* after a superlative, is expressed by **de France**.

B》 Translate these sentences into French.

1   It's the best restaurant in the town for seafood. (les fruits de mer)
2   It's the best area in France for fishing. (la pêche)
3   They're the best harbours in the area for sailing. (la navigation de plaisance)
4   They're the best beaches in France for children. (les enfants)

3.3 Superlative + subjunctive

> C'est le plus beau château que j'aie visité
> **Ce sont les meilleures vacances que j'aie passées.**

○ Look at these examples:

C'est **le plus beau château que j'aie jamais visité**.
It's the most beautiful castle I have ever visited.

Il dit que c'est **le meilleur film qu'il ait jamais vu**.
He says it's the best film he has ever seen.

Both examples have a ***superlative* (le plus beau... /le meilleur...)** followed by a ***relative clause* (que j'aie jamais visité/qu'il ait jamais vu)**. When this happens, the relative clause has to be in the ***subjunctive*** form.

(See pages 49–50 for the superlative and pages 177–9 for the subjunctive.)

C'est le plus beau château que j'aie jamais vu!

» Mme Dupuy was extremely pleased with her holiday. Rephrase what she says using the pattern noted above.

1   Je n'ai jamais vu un si beau coucher de soleil.
    C'est le plus beau coucher de soleil que ___
2   Je n'ai jamais visité un camping si propre.
    C'est le camping le plus propre que ___
3   Je n'ai jamais goûté un plateau de fruits de mer si frais.
    C'est le plateau de fruits de mer le plus frais que ___
4   Je n'ai jamais rencontré un gardien si aimable.
    C'est le gardien le plus aimable que ___
5   Je n'ai jamais fait un séjour si agréable.
    C'est le séjour le plus agréable que ___

3.4 The relative pronouns *qui, que, dont*

> **Il y a beaucoup de campings dont la réputation est excellente et qui ne sont pas trop chers.**
>
> **Tout le monde était sympathique et c'est ça que j'aime avant tout.**

○ There is no separate word for *who* and *which* in French. Whether you use **qui** or **que** depends on the grammatical function of the word. Look at the following examples:

> Je m'entendais bien avec la femme **qui** campait à côté de nous.
> *I got on well with the woman who was camping next to us.*

> Il y avait un restaurant **qui** servait des fruits de mer délicieux.
> *There was a restaurant which served delicious seafood.*

Here **qui** means both *who* and *which*. **Qui** is used because it is the subject of the clause in both cases.

○ Similarly, **que** is used in the next examples to mean both *whom* and *which*:

> Le camping **que** nous avons choisi est très bien aménagé.
> *The campsite which we've chosen is very well laid out.*

> Tous les campeurs **que** j'ai rencontrés étaient très gentils.
> *All the campers whom I met were very kind.*

Que is used because it is the ***direct object*** in both clauses.

○ A rough-and-ready method of deciding whether to use **qui** or **que** is to use **qui** if the next item in the sentence is the verb. If this is not the case, use **que**. Try these examples:

i.   C'est le camping ___ nous avons choisi l'année dernière.
ii. C'est le camping ___ avait une belle piscine.

In the first example, the verb does not come next, therefore **que** is correct. In the second example, the verb does come next, therefore **qui** is correct.

A» Using the rules given above, complete what Mme Dupuy has to say about her holiday by filling the gaps with **qui** or **que**.

1   La tente ___ nous avons louée était trop petite.
2   Nous sommes allés à la plage ___ était à côté du camping.
3   C'est le bruit ___ je n'aime pas.
4   Le repas ___ nous avons pris sur le port était superbe.
5   Ce sont les autres campeurs ___ sont importants pour moi.
6   Les fruits de mer étaient les meilleurs ___ j'aie jamais mangés.
7   C'est Jean-Marc ___ adore la planche à voile.
8   C'est une région ___ je n'ai jamais visitée.

o   **Dont** can mean *of whom, of which, about whom, about which* and *whose*. Look at these examples:

C'est la femme **dont** je parlais hier soir.
It's the woman about whom I was talking last night.

La pollution des plages est un problème **dont** on parle beaucoup.
Coastline pollution is a problem about which we talk a lot.

C'est l'homme **dont** la voiture a été cambriolée.
That's the man whose car was broken into.

B» Use **qui, que, qu'** or **dont** correctly to complete these comments made by tourists about their holidays on the Atlantic coast.

1   Les campeurs ___ on rencontre sont presque tous très sympathiques.
2   Le patron, ___ la femme est anglaise, apprécie beaucoup les campeurs britanniques.
3   Les plages ___ longent la côte sont immenses et très propres.
4   Là-bas, on trouve tous les équipements ___ on pourrait avoir besoin.
5   Les bateaux de plaisance ___ visitent Saint-Gilles créent de l'animation dans ce petit port de pêche.
6   Cette station ___ la plage a une renommée internationale a un certain nombre d'hôtels de luxe.
7   Le musée de voitures anciennes ___ nous avons visité hier était très intéressant.
8   Les dunes ___ la côte est bordée protègent les campings du vent de la mer.

3.5 How to translate *all, everybody, everything*

tout le temps	nous nous sommes tous bien amusés
toute la famille	tout le monde
tous les repas	chaque emplacement
toutes les plages	
tout était calme	

○ There are four forms of the adjective **tout**, meaning *all* or *every*:

tout le temps
all the time

tous les soirs
every evening

toute la journée
the whole day

toutes les semaines
every week

Note especially the spelling of the masculine plural form – **tous**.

A⟩⟩ Use the correct form of **tout** to complete Mme Dupuy's description of the attractions of the Atlantic coast.

Nous allons sur cette côte presque ___ **1** les ans. ___ **2** la famille est très contente d'y aller. ___ **3** le monde aime le sport et il y a ___ **4** sortes d'activités pour satisfaire ___ **5** les âges et ___ **6** les goûts. ___ **7** ces activités attirent un grand nombre d'adeptes. Comme il fait beau presque ___ **8** le temps, on peut passer ___**9** la journée en plein air. ___ **10** les petits Français semblent adorer les activités du Club Mickey. ___ **11** les jours on les voit qui passent ___ **12** la matinée à jouer ensemble. ___ **13** la bande semble se plaire énormément.

○ **Tout le monde** means *everybody* and it always takes a singular verb.

Tout le monde aime la mer.
Everyone likes the seaside.

Au camping, **tout le monde** se parle.
Everyone talks to each other.

○ **Tout** used on its own means *everything*.

> **Tout** était très tranquille.
> *Everything was very quiet.*
>
> **Tout** s'est bien passé.
> *Everything went well.*

Tous and **toutes** used on their own can mean *all*. Look at these examples:

> Nous avons **tous** fait de la planche à voile.
> *We all went windsurfing.*
>
> Elles ont **toutes** mangé des fruits de mer.
> *They all ate seafood.*

B⟩⟩ Mme Dupuy's whole family had a great time on holiday and everybody was prepared to do their bit to make it a real success. Use **tout, tout le monde** or **tous** to complete the passage.

___ **1** a aimé la côte Atlantique. ___ **2** a plu aux enfants: le camping, la plage et toutes les activités. Ils ont ___ **3** fait: de la planche à voile, de l'équitation, du tennis. ___ **4** était exactement comme on l'imaginait. Nous avons ___ **5** participé aux tâches ménagères: ___ **6** a fait les courses à tour de rôle. Un jour, je suis rentrée au camping un peu en retard et ___ **7** était prêt. Ils avaient ___ **8** préparé. Bref, nous avons ___ **9** fait un bon séjour là-bas et je crois que ___ **10** voudrait y retourner l'année prochaine.

○ If you want to express the idea of *every* more emphatically than with **tous**, use **chaque** with a singular noun.

> **Chaque** campeur est responsable de sa voiture et de ses affaires.
> *Each and every camper is responsible for his car and his possessions.*

3.6 Expressions of quantity + *de*

> **beaucoup de** campings
> **un certain nombre de** grands hôtels
> **très peu de** repas
> **la plupart des** campings
> **la plupart du** temps

○ A lot of expressions of quantity are followed by **de**. Look at these examples:

Il y a **beaucoup de** campings sur cette côte.
There are a lot of campsites on this coast.

Il y a **un certain nombre de** grands hôtels.
There are quite a few big hotels.

Il y a **tant de** belles plages.
There are so many good beaches.

Il y a **énormément de** choses à faire.
There are loads of things to do.

○ All the above expressions of quantity follow the same pattern:

expression of quantity + de + noun.

○ La plupart (*most*) is different, and follows this pattern: **la plupart + (de + article) + noun**.

la plupart du temps
most of the time

la plupart des campeurs
most (of the) campers

≫ Use **d', de, du, de la**, or **des** to complete this text about accommodation and things to do on the Atlantic coast.

Très peu ___ **1** touristes fréquentent les hôtels. Un certain nombre ___ **2** estivants louent un appartement mais la plupart ___ **3** visiteurs profitent du grand nombre ___ **4** campings qu'il y a dans la région. On a l'impression que la plupart ___ **5** Français y viennent avec leurs enfants et cela se comprend puisqu'il y a tant ___ **6** activités pour les jeunes. Il y a beaucoup ___ **7** clubs et ___ **8** écoles où ils peuvent apprendre à faire de la voile ou de la planche à voile.

La plupart ___ **9** campeurs aiment passer autant ___ **10** temps que possible à profiter du soleil et de l'air vivifiant de cette côte. Un certain nombre ___ **11** campings ont une piscine mais la plupart ___ **12** plages ne sont pas dangereuses et les enfants peuvent s'y baigner en toute sécurité.

3.7 The perfect tense

> j'ai passé de bonnes vacances   **ils ont fait de la planche à voile**
> je suis allé à la mer   ils sont allés à la mer
> je me suis bien amusé   **ils se sont baignés**

○ The perfect tense is used to describe what happened or has happened in the past. For most verbs, the perfect tense is made up of the *present tense of avoir* + *the past participle*. Look at the different forms of the perfect tense of **manger** given in the following dialogue:

– **Vous n'avez pas mangé** au camping hier soir?
– Non, **nous avons mangé** au restaurant sur le port de Saint-Gilles.
– Qu'est-ce que **tu as mangé**?
– Moi, **j'ai mangé** une sole énorme. **Sylvie a mangé** des fruits de mer superbes! Et **les garçons ont mangé** un bifteck-frites.

○ The past participles of regular verbs are as follows:
  -er verbs
  manger → mangé
  -ir verbs
  finir → fini
  -re verbs
  attendre → attendu

A⟩⟩ Write down the perfect tense of the following verbs for the person given in brackets.

1 choisir (ils)
2 jouer (tu)
3 vendre (je)
4 dîner (nous)
5 acheter (je)
6 attendre (elle)
7 louer (nous)
8 finir (vous)

○ A number of verbs have irregular past participles. Look at the following table. Here they are given with the **je** form of the perfect tense. Test yourself by writing down the infinitive form and then giving the **je** form of the perfect tense.

Infinitive		Past participle with j'ai	Similar verbs
avoir	*to have*	j'ai **eu**	
boire	*to drink*	j'ai **bu**	
conduire	*to drive*	j'ai **conduit**	-uire verbs
connaître	*to know*	j'ai **connu**	-aître verbs (except naître)
courir	*to run*	j'ai **couru**	
craindre	*to fear*	j'ai **craint**	peindre (peint) éteindre (éteint) atteindre (atteint) joindre (joint)
croire	*to believe*	j'ai **cru**	
devoir	*to have to*	j'ai **dû**	recevoir (reçu) apercevoir (aperçu)
dire	*to say*	j'ai **dit**	-dire verbs
écrire	*to write*	j'ai **écrit**	décrire
être	*to be*	j'ai **été**	
faire	*to do/make*	j'ai **fait**	-faire verbs
lire	*to read*	j'ai **lu**	élire
mettre	*to put*	j'ai **mis**	-mettre verbs
ouvrir	*to open*	j'ai **ouvert**	couvrir (couvert) découvrir (découvert) offrir (offert) souffrir (souffert)
pouvoir	*to be able to*	j'ai **pu**	
prendre	*to take*	j'ai **pris**	-prendre verbs
rire	*to laugh*	j'ai **ri**	sourire
savoir	*to know*	j'ai **su**	
suivre	*to follow*	j'ai **suivi**	poursuivre
tenir	*to hold*	j'ai **tenu**	-tenir verbs
vivre	*to live*	j'ai **vécu**	survivre
voir	*to see*	j'ai **vu**	
vouloir	*to want to*	j'ai **voulu**	

○ A small number of verbs form the perfect tense with **être** i.e. *the present tense of être + the past participle*, for example: aller → **je suis allé(e)** (I went).

The following verbs all use **être** in the perfect tense. Note that any irregular past participles are given in brackets. Test yourself by writing out the infinitives of the verbs and then giving the **je** form of the perfect tense.

arriver	*to arrive*
partir	*to leave*
entrer	*to come in*
	(also rentrer to return)
sortir	*to go out*
aller	*to go*
venir (venu)	*to come*
	(also revenir to come back, devenir to become)
monter	*to go up*
descendre	*to go down*
retourner	*to return*
rester	*to stay/remain*
tomber	*to fall*
naître (né)	*to be born*
mourir (mort)	*to die*
passer	*to pass (only takes être when a verb of motion)*

○ The forms of **être verbs** (example: **arriver**) are:

je suis arriv**é**	nous sommes arriv**és**
tu es arriv**é**	vous êtes arriv**és**
on/il est arriv**é**	ils sont arriv**és**
elles est arriv**ée**	elles sont arriv**ées**

○ Note that if the speakers are female, the forms will be:

je suis arriv**ée**	nous sommes arriv**ées**
tu es arriv**ée**	vous êtes arriv**ées**

○ If **vous** is the polite form referring to one person, then use **vous êtes arrivé** (masculine) or **vous êtes arrivée** (feminine).

B ›› Write out the perfect tense of these être verbs.

1	aller (elle)	**5**	monter (elle)
2	partir (ils)	**6**	rester (nous)
3	arriver (nous)	**7**	tomber (il)
4	descendre (elles)	**8**	rentrer (ils)

C)》 Translate the text below into French.

This summer we went to the Atlantic coast. We stayed on a campsite near Les Sables-d'Olonne. The boys went with me at the end of July but my husband stayed in Paris for a week. He finally arrived on August 7th. My sister came to Les Sables-d'Olonne towards the end of the month. She stayed in a hotel and we all went out together several times. Finally we all went back to Paris at the end of August.

○ All reflexive verbs form the perfect tense with **être** i.e. *the present tense of être + the past participle*. With **être** verbs there is an agreement on the past participle. Look at these examples:

– **Tu t'es** bien **amusé** aujourd'hui, Nicolas?
Have you enjoyed yourself today, Nicolas?

– Ce matin, **je me suis baigné** à la piscine. Sophie et papa **se sont amusés** à la plage. Maman **s'est reposée** à la maison.
I swam in the pool this morning. Sophie and Dad enjoyed themselves on the beach. Mum had a rest back at the house.

– L'après-midi, **nous nous sommes promenés** en voiture.
In the afternoon we went out in the car.

– **Vous vous êtes** bien **amusés**?
Did you enjoy yourselves?

– Oui, **nous avons visité** un musée d'automobiles anciennes.
Yes, we visited a classic car museum.

D)》 Write down the perfect tense of the following reflexive verbs for the person given in brackets.

1 se lever (je)
2 se baigner (il)
3 se promener (nous)
4 s'amuser (ils)
5 se reposer (elle)
6 se coucher (vous)

○ Remember that with **être** verbs there is an agreement between the past participle and the subject of the sentence, whereas with **avoir** verbs there is no such agreement.

E》 Complete what Mme Dupuy has to say about her holiday by putting the verbs in brackets into the perfect tense. Remember to make the necessary agreements.

Nous (ALLER **1**) sur la côte Atlantique et nous (FAIRE **2**) du camping. Nous y (RESTER **3**) 15 jours. Les enfants (S'AMUSER **4**). Ils (SE BAIGNER **5**), ils (ALLER **6**) à la pêche et ils (ESSAYER **7**) la planche à voile. Sophie et Anne (SE PROMENER **8**) à cheval. Nous (MANGER **9**) sur la plage une ou deux fois, et le soir du 14 juillet, nous (DÎNER **10**) dans un restaurant près du port.

3.8 *Venir de* + infinitive

Je viens de faire développer nos photos.

○ **Venir de** is used to convey the idea that an action has just happened. Look carefully at the examples below, especially the use of the present tense of **venir**.

Je **viens de** téléphoner à l'agence de voyages.
I have just phoned the travel agency.

On **vient de** confirmer notre réservation.
They have just confirmed our reservation.

》 Replace the whole of the underlined sections by the correct form of **venir de**. Then translate this version into English.

1 Georges? <u>Il est sorti tout à l'heure</u> pour aller faire de la planche à voile.

2 Cet été les Leblanc sont allés dans le Midi: <u>ils ont acheté</u> une villa là-bas <u>il y a trois ou quatre mois</u>.

3 – Vous allez au restaurant en ville ce soir?
– Non. <u>Nous avons déjà dîné</u> au camping.

4 – Tu as réservé une place au camping?
– Oui, <u>je leur ai téléphoné tout à l'heure</u>.

5 – Tu as bonne mine, toi!
– Oui, <u>je suis rentré</u> de vacances <u>hier</u>.

○ Note the use of the imperfect of **venir de** in the example below.

Je **venais de** finir mon petit déjeuner
I had just finished my breakfast.

3.9 Perfect or imperfect

Nous sommes allés à la mer.
Il faisait très chaud.
Ils se sont baignés même si l'eau était plutôt froide.

○ The *perfect tense* is used if the action of the verb took place once
or for a specific and limited time:

Nous **sommes allés** aux Sables-d'Olonne le 30 juillet.
We went to Les Sables-d'Olonne on July 30th.

Ce jour-là, Aurélie **a fait** de la planche à voile pendant six
heures.
That day Aurélie went windsurfing for six hours.

○ The *imperfect tense* is used to describe what was generally true in
a given situation:

Ce jour-là, il **faisait** très chaud.
That day it was very hot.

Tout le monde **se baignait**.
Everybody was swimming.

○ The imperfect tense is also used to talk about what people used to
do in the past frequently:

Quand **j'étais jeune, je me baignais** tous les jours.
When I was young, I used to go swimming every day.

Je **passais** beaucoup de temps sur la plage.
I spent (used to spend) a lot of time on the beach.

○ Look at the following examples. The imperfect tense is used to
describe what someone was doing when something else happened.
The perfect tense is used to describe what it was that happened.

Un jour, **je nageais** à 50 mètres de la côte quand un hors-
bord est passé à 2 mètres de moi.
*I was swimming 50 metres from the coast when a speed-boat went
past a couple of metres from me.*

Hier, Georges **faisait** de la planche à voile quand une vedette
a failli le heurter.
Yesterday, Georges was windsurfing when a motor-launch nearly hit him.

》 Complete this account of a holiday by putting the verbs into the perfect or the imperfect, as appropriate.

Cette année, nous (PASSER **1**) nos vacances sur la côte Atlantique. Autrefois, on (ALLER **2**) tous les ans dans le Midi mais un jour on (FAIRE **3**) une mauvaise expérience. Cette année-là nous (FAIRE **4**) du camping près de la Garde-Freinet. Un jour, nous (DÉCIDER **5**) de visiter St. Tropez. Nous (MONTER **6**) à la citadelle d'où il y (AVOIR **7**) une très belle vue, nous (VISITER **8**) le musée maritime et naturellement, nous (SE PROMENER **9**) sur le port. Vers sept heures, nous (REPARTIR **10**) pour le camping mais comme nous (APPROCHER **11**) de la Garde-Freinet, nous (VOIR **12**) un nuage de fumée noire à l'ouest de la ville, là où (SE TROUVER **13**) notre camping. Nous (CONTINUER **14**) notre chemin mais bientôt nous (DEVOIR **15**) nous arrêter. Un peu plus loin, la route (ÊTRE **16**) coupée par les flammes. Tous les arbres (BRÛLER **17**). On nous (DIRE **18**) que les pompiers (ESSAYER **19**) de maîtriser le feu et que des avions (DÉVERSER **20**) de l'eau sur l'incendie mais le vent (SOUFFLER **21**) très fort et le feu (SE PROPAGER **22**) rapidement. On nous (CONSEILLER **23**) de faire demi-tour. Nous (ÊTRE **24**) si inquiets que nous (DÉCIDER **25**) de passer la nuit dans un hôtel...

Le lendemain, quand nous (RENTRER **26**) au camping, tous les arbres aux alentours (ÊTRE **27**) calcinés* et on (AVOIR **28**) l'impression que le camping aussi (RISQUER **29**) un jour d'être atteint par un incendie. Voilà pourquoi nous (DÉCIDER **30**) de ne plus faire de camping dans le Midi.

* = brûlés

Talking about future plans and asking questions

Je pourrai travailler comme baby-sitter!

A young French student talks about his career plans and his extended working-holiday in Great Britain.

Jérôme:	Et toi, Pierre, **qu'est-ce que tu feras** après le bac?	4.7 / 4.1
Pierre:	Je ne sais pas exactement. Normalement, **on veut** travailler dans une agence de publicité	4.5
	ou **devenir journaliste** à la télévision, mais moi, en ce moment, je ne sais pas	4.9
	précisément **ce que je voudrais faire**.	4.7
Jérôme:	**Tu feras des études universitaires**?	4.1 / 4.6
Pierre:	Je ne crois pas. Je n'aime pas tellement le travail scolaire. Je crois que **je réussirai** mon	4.1
	bac **si je travaille** plus dur mais c'est tout.	4.2

Jérôme:	Mais **qu'est-ce que tu voudrais faire** dans la vie?	4.6 / 4.7
Pierre:	Je ne sais pas **ce qui m'intéresse. Tout ce que je sais**, c'est que le travail de bureau ne m'attire pas du tout. Si je peux, **je travaillerai** pour une société jeune et dynamique, **je voyagerai**, **je rencontrerai** toutes sortes de gens... En tout cas, cet été quand **j'aurai réussi** mon bac, **j'espère aller** en Grande-Bretagne. À Noël **j'aurai passé** trois ou quatre mois là-bas et **quand je reviendrai**, **je parlerai** anglais comme un Anglais!	4.7 4.1 4.1 4.3 4.5 4.3 4.2 / 4.1
Jérôme:	**Et tu as les moyens de te payer un tel séjour**?	4.4
Pierre:	J'ai demandé à mon correspondant Nick de m'aider. Il a dit qu'**il pourrait me trouver** des petits jobs là-bas à Brighton. **Je pourrai livrer** des journaux ou du lait, **travailler comme serveur** dans un restaurant de fast-food ou **comme baby-sitter. Je suis prêt à faire** n'importe quoi pour gagner un peu d'argent, **ce qui me permettra de vivre** sans dépendre de personne. **Tout ce qu'il me faut**, c'est un lit, un peu d'argent et des copains.	4.5 4.1 4.8 4.4 4.7 4.7
Jérôme:	**Ce ne sera pas** très marrant.	4.1 / 4.7
Pierre:	Je ne suis pas d'accord. **Cela me permettra d'entendre** toutes sortes d'accents et **quand je sortirai** le week-end avec Nick **je pourrai parler** anglais avec ses copains. Mais on a assez parlé de moi. **Quels sont tes projets** à toi pour les grandes vacances?	4.8 / 4.1 4.2 4.1 4.7

4.1 The future tense

je travaillerai	je serai	je ferai
je réussirai	j'aurai	**je pourrai**
j'apprendrai	j'irai	**je reviendrai**

O The future tense is used to talk about what is going to happen in the future. In English the words *will* and *shall* are used to convey this idea. In French future endings are added to the infinitives of regular verbs. Look at these examples:

> travailler → **je travaillerai** dur
> *I'll work hard*

> finir → **je finirai** mes examens demain
> *I'll finish my exams tomorrow*

> prendre → **je prendrai** un emploi à temps partiel
> *I'll get a part-time job*

Note that regular **-re** verbs drop the **-e** before the ending is added.

O There is just one set of endings for the future tense. Here is the future tense of the verb **finir**:

> je finir**ai**
> tu finir**as**
> il/elle/on finir**a**
> nous finir**ons**
> vous finir**ez**
> ils/elles finir**ont**

Note that the endings follow the same pattern as the endings of the verb **avoir** in the present tense.

○ A number of important verbs are irregular in the future tense – the endings are the same as those listed above, but the stem needs to be learned:

aller	→ j'irai	*I'll go*
avoir	→ j'aurai	*I'll have*
devoir	→ je devrai	*I'll have to*
envoyer	→ j'enverrai	*I'll send*
être	→ je serai	*I'll be*
faire	→ je ferai	*I'll do*
mourir	→ je mourrai	*I'll die*
pouvoir	→ je pourrai	*I'll be able to*
savoir	→ je saurai	*I'll know*
venir*	→ je viendrai	*I'll come*
voir	→ je verrai	*I'll see*
vouloir	→ je voudrai	*I'll want*
il faut	→ il faudra	*It will be necessary*

*Note that the following verbs are conjugated like **venir**: **revenir devenir tenir** + all verbs ending in -**tenir** (e.g. **maintenir**).

○ Watch out for minor irregularities:

i. A grave accent is added to **acheter, se lever** and all verbs ending in -**mener** (e.g. se **promener, emmener, amener**, etc.)

acheter	→ j'ach**è**terai	*I'll buy*
se lever	→ je me l**è**verai	*I'll get up*
se promener	→ je me prom**è**nerai	*I'll go for a walk*

ii. Note the following changes with verbs like **appeler** and **jeter**:

appeler	→ j'appe**ll**erai	*I'll call*
jeter	→ je je**tt**erai	*I'll throw*

For the verbs noted above, the minor irregularities occur throughout the future tense.

A》 Give the future tense for the person given in brackets after the following verbs.

1	travailler (tu)	5	passer (elle)
2	prendre (il)	6	payer (je)
3	trouver (nous)	7	parler (vous)
4	finir (elles)	8	gagner (ils)

B⟩⟩ Pierre is looking forward to his holiday in England. The following sentences all show how he can talk about something in the future without actually using the future tense. Rewrite his sentences using the future tense of the verb underlined. For example:

Je vais <u>passer</u> mon bac le mois prochain.
Je **passerai** mon bac le mois prochain.

1 Je voudrais <u>aller</u> en Grande-Bretagne.
2 J'espère pouvoir <u>trouver</u> un emploi.
3 J'ai l'intention de <u>travailler</u> un peu tous les jours.
4 J'espère <u>faire</u> un peu de baby-sitting.
5 Je compte <u>voir</u> beaucoup de matchs de foot.
6 J'espère <u>sortir</u> avec les copains de Nick tous les week-ends.
7 Je veux <u>apprendre</u> à parler couramment l'anglais.
8 Je vais <u>acheter</u> un journal anglais tous les jours.
9 J'espère <u>avoir</u> l'occasion de perfectionner mon anglais.
10 Je sais que je vais <u>devoir</u> travailler dur.
11 Je compte <u>revenir</u> en France en août pour le mariage de ma sœur.
12 Je vais <u>rentrer</u> en France au mois d'octobre.

4.2 *Quand* + future tense

quand j'aurai 20 ans
quand je reviendrai en France

O Look at this example:

Quand je rentrerai en France, **je parlerai** anglais comme un Anglais.
When I come back to France, I shall speak English fluently.

Where the present tense is used in English, the future tense is used in French. Always use the future tense to talk about something that will happen in the future. Here's another example:

Quand **je serai** en Angleterre, **j'achèterai** le Times tous les jours.   (FUTURE)   (FUTURE)
When I am in England, I shall buy the Times every day.
       (PRESENT)   (FUTURE)

A⟩⟩ Translate these sentences into French:

1 When I arrive in Brighton, I'll stay with Nick.
2 When I find a job, I'll look for a room.
3 When I go out at the weekend, I'll be able to speak English with Nick's friends.

○ Other conjunctions of time, such as **dès que** and **aussitôt que** (*as soon as*), **après que** (*after*), **tant que** (*as long as*) and **pendant que** (*while*), **lorsque** (*when*), will be followed by a verb in the future tense if the event is still to happen in the future. For example:

Dès que/Aussitôt que j'aurai assez d'argent, je trouverai une chambre.
As soon as I have enough money, I will find a room.

○ Note that **si** (*if*) does not follow this pattern. With **si** the present tense is used as in English:

Si je vais en Angleterre, je logerai chez mon ami, Nick.
If I go to England, I shall stay with my friend Nick.

B⟩⟩ Pierre is writing to tell his grandmother about his future visit to England. In these sentences taken from his letter, put the verb into the correct tense.

1 Si je (PASSER) trois mois à Brighton, je parlerai très bien l'anglais.
2 Quand j'(AVOIR) un emploi, je gagnerai assez d'argent pour être indépendant.
3 Quand je (ÊTRE) chez Nick, je pourrai faire du baby-sitting pour ses voisins.
4 Si je (PARLER) anglais tout le temps, je ferai des progrès.
5 Si tout (MARCHER) bien, je pourrai y rester plus longtemps.
6 Quand je (SE DÉBROUILLER) tout seul, je mènerai une vie plus indépendante.
7 Quand Nick et ses amis (PARLER) entre eux, je pourrai apprendre toutes sortes d'expressions courantes.
8 Si j'(APPRENDRE) à bien parler anglais ce sera très utile pour mon avenir.
9 Quand j'(HABITER) à Brighton, je pourrai aller passer le week-end à Londres de temps en temps.
10 Si j'(AVOIR) le temps, j'irai visiter l'Écosse et le pays de Galles.

4.3 The future perfect tense

j'aurai réussi mon bac
j'aurai passé 3 ou 4 mois en Grande-Bretagne

○ The future perfect tense conveys what one will have done by a certain time.

> Cet été **j'aurai réussi** mon bac.
> *This summer I will have passed my bac exam.*

> A Noël **j'aurai passé** 3 ou 4 mois en Grande-Bretagne.
> *By Christmas I will have spent 3 or 4 months in Britain.*

○ The tense is formed from the ***future tense of the auxiliary verb*** (**avoir** or **être**) plus the ***past participle***.

> **avoir** verbs: Dans 2 ans **j'aurai terminé** mes études à Toulouse.

> **être** verbs: Dans 4 ans **je serai devenu** homme d'affaires en Grande-Bretagne.

> **reflexive** verbs: Dans 5 ans **je me serai installé** dans un grand appartement à Londres.

》 Pierre thinks about his future and what he **will have achieved** at various points in his life over the next 10 years or so.
Put the verbs in brackets into the appropriate forms.

1 Dans 2 ans je (finir) mes études universitaires.
2 Dans trois ans je (s'installer) à Londres.
3 Dans 4 ans je (apprendre) à bien parler anglais.
4 Dans 5 ans je (se marier).
5 Dans 7 ans ma femme et moi (gagner) beaucoup d'argent.
6 Dans 8 ans nous (aller) travailler à l'étranger, aux Etats-Unis peut-être.
7 Dans 10 ans la vie (devenir) très facile – et peut-être très ennuyeuse!

4.4 Nouns and adjectives + infinitive

> J'aurai l'occasion de gagner un peu d'argent.
> Et je serai content de revoir Nick.
> **Je suis prêt à faire n'importe quelle sorte de travail.**

○ Virtually all nouns are followed by **de + infinitive**. For example:

J'ai **envie d'aller** en Angleterre.
I want to go to England.

Here are some very common examples of this pattern.

avoir le temps de	– *to have time to*
avoir l'occasion de	– *to have the opportunity to*
avoir besoin de	– *to need to*
avoir envie de	– *to want to*
avoir les moyens de	– *to be able to afford to*
avoir le droit de	– *to have the right to, to be allowed to*
prendre la peine de	– *to take the trouble to*
courir le risque de	– *to run the risk of*

○ Most adjectives are followed by **de + infinitive**. For example:

Je suis **heureux de pouvoir** aller en Grande-Bretagne.
I'm happy to be able to go to Great Britain.

Il sera **facile de trouver** un emploi.
It will be easy to find a job.

○ A few adjectives, however, take **à + infinitive**. Those listed below are the most common and need to be learned thoroughly.

prêt(e) à	– *ready to, willing to*
disposé(e) à	– *prepared to*
enclin(e) à	– *inclined to*
résolu(e) à	– *determined to*
décidé(e) à	– *determined to*
lent(e) à	– *slow to*
le premier à/la première à	– *(the) first to*
le dernier à/la dernière à	– *(the) last to*
le seul à/ la seule à	– *(the) only one to*
apte à	– *fit to, liable to*
destiné(e) à	– *intended to, designed to*

71

>> Pierre is phoning his sister to tell her about his plans to go and work in England. Complete what Pierre has to say by filling in the gaps with **de** or **à** where necessary.

– Tu sais bien que je suis résolu ___ **1** aller en Grande-Bretagne.

– Oui, je suis sûr ___ **2** trouver un emploi, parce que je suis prêt ___ **3** faire n'importe quoi! Je sais aussi que Brighton est une grande station balnéaire destinée ___ **4** attirer un grand nombre de visiteurs.

– Je cherche des jobs aptes ___ **5** assurer un revenu modeste mais régulier. Je crois que je serai obligé ___ **6** travailler dur.

– Tu te rappelles que Nick était le seul correspondant ___ **7** m'écrire régulièrement. Les autres ont toujours été lents ___ **8** répondre à mes lettres.

– Oui, je serai très content ___ **9** connaître les copains de Nick.

– Pas de problème! Tu sais qu'en cours d'anglais, je suis toujours le premier ___ **10** répondre!

Brighton attire un grand nombre de visiteurs.

4.5 Verbs + infinitive

> **J'espère aller en Grande Bretagne**
> **Je pourrai parler anglais avec ses copains**

○ Remember that when verbs are followed by an infinitive, some need **just the infinitive**, others need **de + infinitive** and others need **à + infinitive**. Look at these examples:

> Pierre **veut être** homme d'affaires
>
> Il a **décidé de** faire un stage d'informatique
>
> Il a **commencé à** apprendre l'anglais

○ Look through the list below. Then cover it up and test yourself by writing out the correct version of the text that follows:

pouvoir	*to be able to*	aimer	*to like to*
savoir	*to know how to*	aimer mieux, préférer	*to prefer to*
vouloir	*to want to*	aller	*to be going to*
espérer	*to hope to*	compter	*to intend to*

accepter de	*to agree to*
choisir de	*to choose to*
offrir de	*to offer to*
décider de	*to decide to*
essayer de	*to try to*
s'efforcer de	*to strive to*
entreprendre de	*to undertake to*
envisager de	*to think of*
promettre de	*to promise to*

passer son temps à	*to spend time...*
perdre son temps à	*to waste time...*
chercher à	*to try to*
commencer à	*to begin to*
consentir à	*to agree to*
contribuer à	*to help to*
réussir à	*to manage to*
tenir à	*to be keen to*
apprendre à	*to learn to*
s'attendre à	*to expect to*

》 Read what Pierre has written about his future plans. Fill in the gaps with **de** or **à** where necessary.

J'ai décidé ___ **1** aller en Grande-Bretagne cet été. J'ai choisi ___ **2** y aller parce que je préfère ___ **3** parler anglais avec de vrais Anglais. Un ami a offert ___ **4** me trouver un emploi à Brighton et je compte ___ **5** y passer deux ou trois mois. Je m'efforce déjà ___ **6** lire des magazines anglais mais maintenant je cherche ___ **7** améliorer mon anglais parlé. Je m'attends ___ **8** faire des progrès rapides en vivant là-bas. Cela va contribuer ___ **9** me préparer pour la vie du travail. Je compte ___ **10** travailler pour une société dynamique et j'espère ___ **11** pouvoir choisir l'emploi qui me convient. Je n'aimerais pas ___ **12** perdre mon temps___ **13** faire un travail routinier. J'espère ___ **14** réussir ___ **15** trouver un emploi vraiment enrichissant. Je ne peux pas ___ **16** envisager ___ **17** passer ma vie ___ **18** faire quelque chose d'ennuyeux! Je vais aussi ___ **19** essayer ___ **20** faire un stage d'informatique l'année prochaine. Il est essentiel ___ **21** savoir utiliser un ordinateur et je tiens beaucoup ___ **22** apprendre ___ **23** en utiliser un aussitôt que possible. Mon père a consenti ___ **24** me payer le stage et j'ai promis ___ **25** prendre enfin mes études au sérieux!

4.6 Question forms and question words

Tu feras des études universitaires?
Est-ce que tu feras des études universitaires?
Feras-tu des études universitaires?

○ There are various ways of asking questions in contemporary spoken French. Perhaps the most common is to use a statement either with a rising intonation or with a *question word* added:

Tu vas trouver un emploi à Brighton?
Are you going to get a job in Brighton?

L'avion part à **quelle** heure?
What time does the plane leave?

Ça s'écrit **comment**, l'adresse de ton ami?
How is your friend's address spelt?

This form of question can be used only in spoken French or in informal written French (for example, when you're writing to a close friend).

○ Note the following question words:

Où?	*Where?*	Combien?	*How many?*
Quand?	*When?*		*How much?*
A quelle heure?	*When?*	Combien de temps?	*How long?*
Comment?	*How?*	Pourquoi?	*Why?*

○ In more formal contexts there are two question forms available. Firstly, you can invert the verb and the subject:

> **Pourriez-vous** m'écrire une lettre de recommandation pour un employeur éventuel?
> *Could you write me a letter of recommendation for a potential employer?*

> Ton ami Nick, où **habite-t-il**?
> *Where does your friend Nick live?*

> Quelles matières **a-t-il étudiées** à l'université?
> *What subjects did he study at university?*

In the last two examples, note the addition of **-t-** to bridge the gap between the two vowels (a il → **a-t-il**).

○ Note also that if there is a noun as subject of the verb in this inverted type of question, the appropriate pronoun is used with the verb:

> Pourquoi **Pierre veut-il** aller en Grande-Bretagne?
> *Why does Pierre want to go to Britain?*

> **Ses parents vont-ils** lui donner de l'argent?
> *Are his parents going to give him some money?*

○ Secondly, you can use **est-ce que?** to avoid the inversion:

> **Que vas-tu** faire? → **Qu'est-ce que tu vas** faire?

> **Comment espère-t-il** gagner sa vie? → **Comment est-ce qu'il espère** gagner sa vie?

>> Look at the list of informal questions below. Turn these into formal questions, using firstly the **inversion** and secondly the **est-ce qu...?** version.

1 Tu vas habiter où en Grande-Bretagne?
2 Tu espères gagner combien d'argent?
3 Tu vas rentrer en France quand?
4 Pierre part pour Brighton quand?
5 Il va voyager comment?
6 La famille de Nick peut héberger Pierre longtemps?
7 Tu veux trouver quelle sorte de job?
8 Pierre parle bien le français?

4.7 How to translate *what*

– Qu'est-ce qui t'intéresse?
– **Je ne sais pas ce qui m'intéresse vraiment.**
– Qu'est-ce que tu veux faire dans la vie?
– Je ne sais pas encore ce que je veux faire.
– **Quels sont tes projets?**
– Quels diplômes as-tu?

○ *What* in a direct question (i.e. when there is a question mark at the end of the sentence, as in *'What interests Pierre?'*) is translated as follows:

> **Qu'est-ce qui** intéresse Pierre comme emploi?
> *What interests Pierre in the job line?*

> **Qu'est-ce que** tu vas faire après le bac? OR
> **Que** vas-tu faire après le bac?
> *What are you going to do after the bac?*

Use **Qu'est-ce qui** when *what* is the subject of the sentence, and **Qu'est-ce que** or **Que** when *what* is the object of the sentence.

○ *What* in an indirect question (i.e. when there is no question mark at the end of the sentence, as in *'I don't know what interests Pierre'*) is translated as follows:

> Je ne sais pas **ce qui** m'intéresse.
> *I don't know what interests me.*

> Je ne sais pas **ce que** je voudrais faire.
> *I don't know what I would like to do.*

Use **ce qui** when *what* is the subject of the sentence, and **ce que** when *what* is the object of the sentence.

○ When used with a preposition *what* is translated as follows:

En quoi puis-je vous aider?
In what way can I help you?

De quoi parlez-vous?
What are you talking about?

À quoi servent les études supérieures?
What is the use of higher education?

De quoi s'agit-il?
What's it all about?

○ When used with a noun, *what* is used as an adjective and is translated as follows:

Quel emploi as-tu choisi?
What job have you chosen?

Quelle expérience du travail as-tu?
What work experience have you got?

Quels sont tes projets pour l'été?
What are your plans for the summer?

Quelles matières préfères-tu au lycée?
What subjects do you prefer at school?

○ **Ce qui** and **ce que** (see above) can also be used to refer to an idea, rather than to a particular noun. Look at these examples:

Je pourrai gagner un peu d'argent, **ce qui** me permettra de vivre sans dépendre de personne.
I'll be able to earn a little money, which (the earning of the money) will allow me to live independently.

Ma mère me demande tout le temps si j'ai bien mangé, **ce que** je déteste.
My mother asks me all the time if I've had enough to each, which (her asking all the time) I hate.

Use **ce qui** when the idea referred to is the subject of the sentence, and **ce que** when the idea referred to is the object of the sentence.

A)> Complete this conversation between Pierre and his friend, Manon, by filling the gaps with **qu'est-ce qui, qu'est-ce que, ce qui,** or **ce que**.

Manon: ___ **1** tu vas faire quand tu arriveras à Brighton?

Pierre: Nick va m'expliquer ___ **2** je dois faire pour trouver une chambre.

Manon: Et ___ **3** va arriver si tu ne trouves pas d'emploi?

Pierre: Nick va me téléphoner ce week-end pour me dire ___ **4** il a trouvé comme emploi.

Manon: ___ **5** tes parents ont dit?

Pierre: ___ **6** inquiète le plus ma mère, c'est ___ **7** je vais manger quand je serai en Grande-Bretagne! Pour moi, ___ **8** est important, c'est que je dois faire beaucoup de progrès en anglais.

B)> Now complete this conversation between Pierre and another friend, Alain, by filling in the gaps with **qu'est-ce qui, qu'est-ce que, ce qui, ce que, quoi,** or the correct form of **quel**.

Pierre: Tu sais ___ **1** me donne envie d'aller en Grande-Bretagne? ___ **2** me plaît, c'est l'idée de vivre comme les Anglais.

Alain: Mais de ___ **3** vas-tu vivre en Angleterre? ___ **4** sorte de travail espères-tu faire? ___ **5** tu vas gagner comme salaire? Nick, ___ **6** il fait comme travail?

Pierre: Tant de questions! Je sais que les premiers jours, je pourrai dépenser ___ **7** mes parents vont me donner, et ensuite ce sera à moi de me débrouiller!... De ___ **8** ris-tu? Tu penses à ___ **9** mes parents vont dire?

Alain: Écoute bien ___ **10** je vais te dire. On ne sait jamais ___ **11** peut arriver à l'étranger!

4.8 *Ce* or *cela*?

Ce ne sera pas marrant.
Cela me permettra d'entendre toutes sortes d'accents.

○ Look at these examples of how to use **ce** and **cela** *(this/that)*:

Ce ne sera pas marrant.
That won't be much fun.

Je voudrais passer quelques jours chez vous si **cela** ne vous dérange pas trop.
I would like to come and stay for a few days if that's OK by you.

The rule is to use **ce** with the verb **être** and **cela** with all other verbs.

○ In speech, **cela** is usually shortened to **ça**.

Ça va?	*Is that all right?*
Ça ne fait rien.	*That doesn't matter.*
Ça ne me dit rien.	*That doesn't appeal to me.*

○ Both **ce** and **cela** will also convey the meaning *it* if *it* refers to a general idea.

Il faut écouter attentivement si on veut tout comprendre. **Ce** n'est pas facile du tout.
You have to listen carefully if you want to understand everything. It's not at all easy.

Si je gagne un peu d'argent, **cela** me permettra d'être indépendant.
If I earn a bit of money, it will allow me to be independent.

» **Pierre is very keen to improve his English and to improve his career prospects. Use ce or cela as appropriate to complete what he has to say.**

Travailler dans une banque? Non, ___ **1** ne m'attire pas. ___ **2** est trop routinier. Si je réussis à mon bac, ___ **3** me permettra d'aller à l'université plus tard. Travailler pour une grande société internationale, ___ **4** serait vraiment passionnant. J'aurai 2000 francs que mon père va me donner. ___ **5** me donnera le temps de chercher un emploi. Quand on travaille comme serveur, on rencontre toutes sortes de gens. ___ **6** est très intéressant pour un étudiant en langues. Vivre dans une ambiance vraiment anglaise, ___ **7** sera fascinant mais ___ **8** me fait un peu peur aussi. Vivre dans un pays étranger, ___ **9** vous aide à bien connaître la langue. Si je vois un film anglais à la télévision, ___ **10** me donne tout de suite envie d'aller en Grande-Bretagne.

4.9 How to talk about jobs

devenir journaliste
travailler comme serveur
comme babysitter

○ Look at these examples and note the difference between the English and French usage:

Pierre veut **être homme d'affaires**.
Pierre wants to be a business man.

Normalement on veut **devenir journaliste**.
Normally people want to be journalists.

Nick est étudiant en sciences économiques à Brighton.
Nick is an economics student in Brighton.

Note that the indefinite article (**un** or **une**) is omitted in French when talking about what job someone has.

A》 Below is a list of words which refer to the status or occupation of various people. Fit them appropriately into the sentences below the list.

fils unique	coiffeuse	chauffeur de taxi
comptable	lycéen	professeur
chômeur	serveur	
programmeur	plombier	

1   Pierre n'a ni frère ni sœur. Il est ___.
2   Il s'intéresse à l'informatique mais il ne voudrait pas devenir ___.
3   En ce moment, il est en terminale: il est ___ à Paris.
4   Sa mère voudrait que Pierre soit ___ comme elle mais Pierre n'est pas très fort en maths.
5   Colin, le frère de Nick, travaille dans le bâtiment comme ___.
6   Un autre frère travaille comme ___ chez McDonald.
7   Sa sœur qui est ___ travaille dans un salon de coiffure à Hove.
8   Son père est ___. Ses affaires marchent bien, surtout l'été quand il conduit beaucoup de clients à Gatwick.
9   Sa mère est ___ d'éducation physique.
10 Aucun membre de la famille n'est ___ et Pierre est sûr qu'il pourra trouver un emploi.

B》 Translate the following sentences into French.

1   Jérôme wants to be a business man.
2   He is still a student.
3   He works as a waiter during the holidays.
4   His father is a teacher.
5   His mother is a journalist.
6   His sister has already found a job. She works as an accountant.

Normalement on veut devenir journaliste.

Giving advice and instructions

Accélérez doucement!

A driving-instructor gives some last-minute advice to a learner-driver the day before the test.

La monitrice d'une auto-école parle.

– Bon. Je viens de vous donner **votre dernière leçon avant**	5.7 / 5.5
l'épreuve de conduite. Et maintenant, **je vous demande**	
d'écouter attentivement ce que je vais vous dire.	5.1 / 5.9
Naturellement, **j'encourage toujours mes élèves à**	5.9 / 5.2
conduire avec prudence. **Je leur dis d'accélérer** et de	5.1
freiner **doucement** mais **normalement**, **la première fois**	5.9 / 5.7
qu'ils se trouvent seuls au volant, ils conduisent **avec une**	5.9
imprudence incroyable...	

Alors j'ai quelques bons conseils à vous donner. D'abord, **ne brûlez jamais les feux**. Là-bas, au carrefour, **vous auriez dû vous arrêter** au feu orange. **C'est vraiment très dangereux**, ce que vous avez fait là.

5.3
5.6 / 5.8

Et puis, quand on conduit, **il faut constamment** faire attention. **Il est essentiel, par exemple, d'utiliser** son rétroviseur **avant de dépasser** un autre véhicule. **Sinon on risque de provoquer un grave accident.**

5.12 / 5.9
5.8
5.5
5.12

Réussir l'épreuve **c'est bien**, mais cela ne suffit pas: pendant **les six premiers mois après avoir obtenu** son permis de conduire, **on doit apprendre à bien conduire**. **C'est pour cette raison qu'on ne permet pas aux nouveaux titulaires de conduire** à plus de 90 kilomètres à l'heure...

5.8 / 5.9
5.7 / 5.4
5.12 / 5.9
5.8 / 5.1

Je vous conseille surtout de ne jamais rouler trop **vite** ou **de façon irresponsable**. **Ne vous inquiétez pas** si les autres vous dépassent... En arrivant à un carrefour ou en approchant d'un rond-point, **vous devriez ralentir** en freinant **légèrement**. Et si **vous faites installer** un lecteur de CD dans votre nouvelle voiture, **n'écoutez pas** la musique au lieu de regarder **attentivement** ce qui se passe autour de vous.

5.1 / 5.9
5.9 / 5.3

5.6 / 5.12
5.9 / 5.11
5.3
5.9

Bon. Je crois que vous aurez le permis demain. Mais **n'allez pas penser** que vous êtes le meilleur conducteur du monde! Alors, à demain! Et bonne chance!

5.3 / 5.12

5.1 *Demander à quelqu'un de faire*

> Je conseille à mes élèves de conduire avec prudence.
> **Je leur dis d'accélérer et de freiner doucement.**

○ The pattern **verb + à + person + de + verb** must be followed when using **demander** to translate *to ask somebody to do something*:

> Souvent les jeunes **demandent à leurs parents de leur acheter** une voiture.
> *Young people often ask their parents to buy them a car.*

Below is a list of verbs which follow the "demander" pattern.

dire à quelqu'un + de
to tell someone to do

promettre à quelqu'un + de
to promise someone to do

permettre à quelqu'un + de
to allow someone to do

défendre à quelqu'un + de
interdire à quelqu'un + de
to forbid someone to do

conseiller à quelqu'un + de
to advise someone to do

commander à quelqu'un + de
ordonner à quelqu'un + de
to order someone to do

recommander à quelqu'un + de
to recommend that someone should do

A》 The instructions given during the lesson are listed below. Rephrase the sentences, saying what the instructor asked the learner to do:

La monitrice a demandé à son élève de...
1   Attendez le feu vert!
2   Utilisez le rétroviseur plus souvent!
3   Ralentissez en approchant du rond-point!
4   Bouclez la ceinture de sécurité!
5   Faites attention tout le temps!
6   Pensez aux autres automobilistes!
7   Conduisez plus lentement!
8   Prenez moins de risques!

B⟩⟩ Make up similar sentences by using the elements of incomplete sentences below. Add **à, au, aux, d'** or **de** where appropriate, make necessary adjustments and put the verb in brackets into the perfect tense.

1   Martin / (DEMANDER) / son père / acheter une vieille bagnole.

2   La monitrice / (CONSEILLER) / Martin / vérifier l'état des pneus.

3   On / (DIRE) / Martin / rester à l'hôpital.

4   On / (PERMETTRE) / les autres jeunes / rentrer chez eux.

5   Le père de Florence / (ORDONNER) / la jeune fille / ne plus sortir avec Martin

6   Le garagiste / (DIRE) / le jeune homme / faire réparer les dégâts aussi vite que possible.

○   Take care when the **à + noun** is replaced by a *pronoun* (**lui, leur, me, nous etc.**). It is important to continue to use **de** before the infinitive:

> La monitrice a dit à Martin **de conduire** plus lentement.
> *The instructor told Martin to drive more slowly.*

> La monitrice lui a dit **de conduire** plus lentement.
> *The instructor told him to drive more slowly.*

> On a permis **aux jeunes de** rentrer chez eux.
> *They allowed the young people to go home.*

> On **leur** a permis **de** rentrer chez eux.
> *They allowed them to go home.*

C⟩⟩ Write down the pronoun version of the sentences below.

1   On conseille **à l'élève** de ne pas démarrer trop brusquement.

2   On dit **au nouveau titulaire** de conduire avec prudence.

3   Souvent les parents permettent **aux enfants** de conduire la voiture familiale.

4   On demande souvent **à ses parents** d'acheter une voiture d'occasion.

5.2 *Aider quelqu'un à faire*

> J'encourage mes élèves à conduire avec prudence.

○ It is important to distinguish between verbs like **demander** (**demander à quelqu'un de faire**) and verbs like **aider (aider quelqu'un à faire**).

○ The following verbs follow the **aider** pattern:

inviter quelqu'un + à
to invite someone to do

encourager quelqu'un + à
to encourage someone to do

pousser quelqu'un + à
inciter quelqu'un + à
to urge someone to do

autoriser quelqu'un + à
to authorize someone to do

condamner quelqu'un + à
to condemn someone to do

forcer quelqu'un + à
obliger quelqu'un + à
to force someone to do

amener quelqu'un + à
to induce someone to do

conduire quelqu'un + à
to lead someone to do

》 Join up the elements below appropriately.

1   J'ai aidé / beaucoup de jeunes / obtenir le permis de conduire.
2   Je ne permets pas / mes élèves / fumer.
3   J'encourage / mes élèves / utiliser le rétroviseur tout le temps.
4   Au début vous ne devriez pas inviter / vos copains / monter dans votre voiture.
5   On conseille / tous les jeunes / conduire avec prudence.
6   On oblige / tous les débutants / rouler à moins de 90 kilomètres à l'heure.

5.3 The imperative

> Démarrez doucement!   Calmez-vous!
> Ne brûlez jamais les feux!   Ne vous inquiétez pas!

○ To form the imperative (to give someone an order/tell someone what to do), use the **tu, nous** or **vous** form of the present tense of the verb **without** the **tu, nous** or **vous.** For example:

Prends la deuxième à droite!
Take the second on the right!

Essayons cette manœuvre encore une fois!
Let's try that manoeuvre again!

Tournez à gauche!
Turn left!

○ Negative imperatives (telling someone what not to do) follow this pattern:

Ne tournez pas à droite! *Don't turn right!*

○ Note that the **-s** ending of the tu form of **-er** verbs is dropped in the imperative. For example:

present tense:	Tu tournes à droite	*You are turning right*
imperative:	**Tourne** à droite!	*Turn right!*
present tense:	Tu vas tout droit	*You are going straight on*
imperative:	**Va** tout droit!	*Go straight on!*

A⟩⟩ Write down the imperative forms of the verbs below.

When addressing someone as **tu**:
1 Il faut freiner plus doucement.
2 Il est essentiel de conduire avec prudence.
3 Il faut penser aux autres automobilistes.
4 Il est essentiel de changer de vitesse plus tôt.

When conveying the idea of *let's do something*:
5 Est-ce qu'on peut démarrer maintenant?
6 Est-ce qu'on peut prendre la deuxième à gauche?
7 Est-ce qu'on peut faire cette manœuvre encore une fois?
8 Est-ce qu'on peut finir maintenant?

When addressing someone as **vous**:
9 Il faut lire le code de la route très attentivement.
10 Il est essentiel de faire attention tout le temps.
11 Il faut ralentir avant d'arriver à un rond-point.
12 Il est essentiel de partir toujours à temps.

○ To form the imperative of reflexive verbs, follow the rules noted above and note also that the reflexive pronoun is placed after the verb. Look at this example with the verb **se taire** (*to be quiet*):

87

present tense:	vous vous taisez	*you are quiet*
imperative:	**taisez-vous**!	*be quiet!*
present tense:	nous nous taisons	*we are quiet*
imperative:	**taisons-nous**!	*let's be quiet!*

Note that a hyphen is added when the pronoun is placed after the verb.

○ The imperative of **tu forms** is slightly different. Look at this example, again with the verb **se taire** (to be quiet):

present tense:	tu te tais	*you are quiet*
imperative:	**tais-toi**!	*be quiet!*

The reflexive pronoun te is replaced by **toi**.

B》 Write down the imperative forms of the verbs below, using **tu**:

1 Martin, tu dois te dépêcher.
2 Tu dois monter dans la voiture.
3 Tu dois t'installer confortablement.
4 Tu dois vérifier le frein à main et le levier de vitesse.
5 Tu dois te calmer.
6 Tu dois bien te préparer pour l'épreuve.
7 Tu dois te rappeler tous mes conseils.

○ In negative imperatives, the reflexive pronouns are placed before the verb. Compare these examples:

asseyez-vous!	*sit down!*
ne vous asseyez pas!	*don't sit down!*
baignons-nous!	*let's go for a swim!*
ne nous baignons pas!	*let's not go for a swim!*

Note that the hyphen is only added in positive commands when the pronoun comes after the verb.

○ With negative imperatives of **tu** forms, the reflexive pronoun **te** is used – it only changes to **toi** in positive commands:

dépêche-**toi**!	*hurry up!*
ne **te** dépêche pas!	*don't hurry up!*

C)) The instructor is not pleased with the learner's driving this morning. Write out what she tells him not to do – give the negative imperative of the following verbs.

1   se mettre au milieu de la chaussée (vous)
2   s'approcher trop des autres véhicules (vous)
3   s'arrêter trop près du trottoir (vous)
4   se fâcher (vous)
5   se disputer (nous)

D)) The learner's father also has some last-minute advice. Write out what he tells him not to do – give the negative imperative of the following verbs.

1   s'amuser à regarder ce qui se passe dans la rue (tu)
2   s'occuper des erreurs des autres automobilistes (tu)
3   se tromper de vitesse (tu)

5.4 How to translate *after*

> après l'examen audio-visuel
> **après avoir obtenu le permis de conduire**

O   With a noun use **après**:

après l'épreuve de conduite   *after the driving test*

O   With a verb, there are several ways of translating *after*:

i.   When the same person is the subject of both clauses, use **après + *perfect infinitive***. There are different versions of this pattern, depending on whether a verb takes **avoir** or **être** in the perfect tense. Look at these examples:

avoir verbs: **après + avoir + *past participle***. For example:

Après avoir conduit pendant quelques semaines, on fait toutes les manœuvres sans y penser.
After you've driven for a few weeks, you do all the manoeuvres instinctively.

être verbs: **après + être + *past participle***. For example:

Après être monté dans la voiture, on vérifie le frein à main, on ajuste le rétroviseur...
After getting in your car, you check the handbrake, you adjust the mirror...

Reflexive verbs: après + s'être + *past participle*. For example:

Après s'être habitué au maniement de la voiture, il faut apprendre à utiliser la route correctement.
After you've got used to handling the car, you have to learn how to use the road properly.

Note that when **être** is used the past participle must agree with the subject. With reflexive verbs use the correct reflexive pronoun for the subject of the sentence. For example:

Après m'être installé, je...

ii.   When the subjects of the two clauses are different, use **après que**...

Après que j'avais brûlé les feux plusieurs fois, mon père a refusé de m'accompagner.
After I had gone through the red lights several times, my father refused to go out with me any more.

A⟩⟩ Complete the following sentences. Use a suitable **après** construction, and alter the verbs in brackets as appropriate.

1   ___ (CHANGER) la roue, ils se sont remis en route.
2   ___ (RÉUSSIR) à l'examen du code de la route, on peut passer le permis de conduire.
3   ___ (APPRENDRE) à conduire, les jeunes veulent acheter une voiture à eux.
4   ___ la voiture était tombée en panne plusieurs fois, on a décidé de la vendre.
5   ___ ma première leçon, j'ai pensé que je n'obtiendrais jamais mon permis de conduire.
6   ___ Martin avait donné son nom et son adresse, le policier lui a permis de partir.
7   ___ (PRENDRE) un café et ___ (SE REPOSER) un peu, il a pu continuer son chemin.
8   ___ (RÉUSSIR) au permis de conduire, il a demandé à ses parents de lui acheter une voiture.

B⟩⟩ Use the correct form of the verb in brackets. Watch out for agreements!

1   Après (S'INSTALLER) au volant, elle ___
2   Après (VÉRIFIER) le rétroviseur, il ___

3   Après (METTRE) le moteur en marche, elle ___
4   Après (S'ASSURER) qu'il n'y avait pas de danger, elle ___
5   Après (CONDUIRE) pendant une demi-heure, elle ___
6   Après (S'ARRÊTER) au bord du trottoir, ils ___
7   Après (ÉCOUTER) les conseils du moniteur, elle ___
8   Après (PRENDRE) ma première leçon, je ___
9   Après (S'HABITUER) au maniement de la voiture, je ___
10   Après (SORTIR) seul pour la première fois, je ___

5.5 How to translate *before*

avant l'épreuve de conduite
avant de dépasser un autre véhicule

○   With a noun use **avant**:

avant l'épreuve de conduite
before the driving test

○   With a verb, there are two constructions:

i.   When the same person is the subject of both clauses, use
avant de + *infinitive*:

Martin a pris 20 leçons **avant de passer** son permis de
conduire.
Martin had 20 lessons before he took/before taking his driving test.

ii. When the subjects of the two clauses are different people, use
avant que + *subjunctive*.

Avant que le candidat puisse passer l'épreuve de
conduite, l'examinateur lui explique ce qui va se passer.
*Before the candidate can take the driving test, the examiner explains
what will happen.*

A⟩⟩ Use **avant**, **avant de** or **avant que/qu'** as appropriate in the
following sentences.

1   On doit mettre son clignotant ___ changer de voie.
2   ___ on achète une voiture d'occasion, un mécanicien devrait
l'examiner.

3   ___ passer l'épreuve de conduite, on doit passer l'examen du code de la route.

4   ___ arriver au carrefour, le conducteur doit freiner légèrement.

5   On ne peut pas conduire à plus de 90 kilomètres à l'heure ___ la fin de la première année.

6   Le moniteur vous donne toujours beaucoup de conseils ___ on passe le permis.

7   On doit toujours regarder une bonne carte routière ___ partir.

8   ___ changer de vitesse, on doit freiner un peu.

Avant l'épreuve...

5.6 How to translate *ought to do/should do/ought to have done/should have done*

> **Vous devriez ralentir.**
> **Vous auriez dû vous arrêter au feu orange.**

○   The *conditional* of **devoir** is used to convey the idea that one *should/ought to do something,* and the verb expressing what one should do is in the infinitive:

On devrait penser tout le temps aux autres usagers de la route.
You should think about other road-users all the time.

The *conditional* of **devoir** is as follows:

je devrais	nous devrions
tu devrais	vous devriez
il/elle/on devrait	ils/elles devraient

○ The *conditional perfect* of **devoir** is used to convey the idea that one *should have done/ought to have done* something and the verb expressing what one should have done is the infinitive.

On aurait dû prendre la première route à gauche.
We should have taken the first road on the left.

The conditional perfect of **devoir** is as follows:

j'aurais dû	nous aurions dû
tu aurais dû	vous auriez dû
il/elle/on aurait dû	ils/elles auraient dû

》 Rephrase the advice given below, using the conditional or conditional perfect of devoir to say what people should do or should have done.

1 N'oublie pas de regarder dans ton rétroviseur. Tu ___
2 Ne changez pas de voie sans utiliser le clignotant. Vous ne ___
3 Mais tu ne t'es pas arrêté au feu rouge! Tu ___
4 On a oublié d'acheter une bonne carte routière. On ___
5 N'oubliez jamais de boucler votre ceinture avant de partir. Vous ___ toujours
6 Il ne faut jamais rouler vite quand les routes sont mouillées. On ne ___
7 Vous avez traversé le carrefour sans regarder à gauche ni à droite. Vous ___
8 Vous avez brûlé les feux. C'est très dangereux. Vous n'___

Vous avez brûlé les feux rouges!

5.7 *dernier* and *prochain*

la première fois	la semaine dernière
la prochaine fois	l'année prochaine

○ The adjective **dernier/dernière** comes **before** the noun when it conveys the idea of *the last* or *the latest* in a series.

> C'est votre **dernière leçon** avant l'épreuve de conduite.
> *It's your last lesson before the driving test.*

> **Le dernier modèle** de Renault a beaucoup de succès.
> *The latest Renault model is very popular.*

○ The adjective **prochain(e)** meaning the *next in a series*, follows the same pattern.

> Je descends au **prochain** arrêt.
> *I'm getting off at the next stop.*

○ **Dernier/dernière** comes after the noun when it conveys the idea of *the last one before this* (usually with days of the week and with **semaine, mois, an/année**).

> **samedi dernier**   *last Saturday*
> **la semaine dernière**   *last week*
> **le mois dernier**   *last month*
> **l'an dernier, l'année dernière**   *last year*

○ The rule for **prochain(e)** is similar when it is used to mean *the one after this*.

> **samedi prochain**   *next Saturday*
> **l'année prochaine**   *next year*

○ Note that the word order is the opposite to English when **dernier** and **prochain** (and **premier**) are used with numbers:

> au cours des **30 dernières** années
> *during the last 30 years*

> dans les **10 prochaines** années
> *within the next 10 years*

> les **deux premières** leçons
> *the first two lessons*

A〉〉 Add the correct form of **dernier** in its correct position to complete these sentences.

1 C'est la fois que je sors avec lui! (THE LAST TIME)
2 Le garage avait les pièces dont nous avions besoin. (THE LAST GARAGE)
3 J'ai passé mon permis de conduire la semaine des vacances de Pâques. (THE LAST WEEK)
4 Il a acheté une nouvelle voiture le mois. (LAST MONTH)
5 Au cours des cinq années, ils ont sorti trois nouveaux modèles. (THE LAST FIVE YEARS)

B〉〉 Add the correct form of **prochain** in its correct position to complete the following sentences.

1 La semaine, j'espère acheter une nouvelle voiture. (NEXT WEEK)
2 Dans les 20 années, beaucoup de Français vont acheter une voiture. (THE NEXT 20 YEARS)
3 Lundi, j'irai au lycée en voiture pour la première fois. (NEXT MONDAY)

5.8 Impersonal phrases: *il est* or *c'est*?

Il est essentiel d'utiliser son rétroviseur.
C'est très dangereux.

○ The standard pattern in formal French is:

Il est + adjective + de + infinitive
(You will often hear C'est + adjective + de + infinitive in spoken French.)

Il est dangereux de brûler les feux.
Il est difficile de faire attention tout le temps.
Il est formidable d'avoir sa propre voiture.

○ If, however, the idea is complete in itself, **c'est** is used instead. Compare these examples:

– **Il est possible d'avoir** le permis après dix leçons?
– **C'est possible** mais **c'est difficile**.

>> Use **il** or **c'** as appropriate in the following sentences.

_____ (**1**) est essentiel de démarrer doucement. _____ (**2**) est plus prudent aussi.

Avoir sa propre auto, _____ (**3**) est formidable. _____ (**4**) est si facile d'arriver à l'heure prévue.

_____ (**5**) est imprudent de brûler les feux. En fait, _____ (**6**) est vraiment suicidaire.

Conduire avec prudence, _____ (**7**) est moins passionnant mais _____ (**8**) est plus sûr.

_____ (**9**) est important d'obéir aux règles de la route même si _____ (**10**) est un peu embêtant quelquefois.

Prendre des leçons de conduite, _____ (**11**) est cher mais _____ (**12**) est très utile.

○ The same rule applies with phrases like **Il est évident que... Il est vrai que... Il est naturel que...**

Compare these examples:

– **Il est naturel que** les jeunes conducteurs conduisent vite.
– Oui, **c'est naturel** mais **c'est dangereux** – pour eux et pour les autres.

○ A selective check-list of impersonal verbs and phrases

You will already have come across structures where the verb is used only or mainly in the **il** form e.g. il neige, il pleut, il fait beau, il y a, s'il vous plaît. These are called ***impersonal verbs***.

Below is a list of common impersonal verbs. The structures marked **s** will take a verb in the subjunctive: all the others are followed by a verb in the indicative.

il s'agit de (+ infinitive)	*it's a question of*
il arrive que (s)	*it sometimes happens that*
quoiqu'il arrive (s)	*whatever happens*
il convient de (+ infinitive)	*it is advisable/right to*
il est dommage que (s)	*it'a pity that*
il en est ainsi	*this is the way it is*
il en est de même de	*it's the same with*
quoiqu'il en soit	*however that may be*
il fait jour	*it's light*
il fait noir/nuit	*it's dark*
comment se fait-il que...? (s)	*how is it that...?*
il faut (+ infinitive)	*it is necessary to*

il me faut (mille francs)	*I need (1000 francs)*
il faut que (s)	*it is necessary that*
il gèle	*it's freezing*
il manque (deux chaises)	*there are (two chairs) missing*
il me manque (cinquante francs)	*I'm (50 francs) short*
il paraît que (s)	*it appears that*
il se passe (quelque chose de grave)	*(something serious) is going on*
il se peut que (s)	*it is possible that*
il ne me plaît pas de (+ infinitive)	*I don't fancy*
il reste (deux croissants)	*there are (two croissants) left*
il me reste (dix francs)	*I have (10 francs) left*
il ne reste qu'à (+ infinitive)	*all we can do is*
il semble que (s)	*it seems that*
il me semble que	*it seems to me that...*
il suffit de (+ infinitive)	*it is enough to, all you have to do is*
il suffit que (s)	*it is enough that*
il est/se fait tard	*it is getting late*
il est temps que (s)	*it is time that*
il va sans dire que	*it goes without saying that*
il vaut la peine de (+ infinitive)	*it is worthwhile*
il vaut mieux (+ infinitive)	*it is better*
il vaudrait mieux (+ infinitive)	*it would be better*
il n'y a qu'à (+ infinitive)	*all we can do is*
il y a peu de chances que (s)	*it is unlikely that*
il y a de fortes chances que (s)	*it is very likely that*

○ Most adjectives in French can be used with **il est** and an infinitive to convey the idea of *it is (interesting) to, it is (preferable) to* etc. Here are a few examples:

> **Il est intéressant de vivre** à l'étranger.
> **Il est préférable de trouver** un emploi.
> **Il est essentiel de s'adapter** vite au mode de vie étranger.
> **Il est préférable de vivre** dans une famille étrangère.

○ Many adjectives are used with **il est** and **que** to convey *it is (certain) that..., it is (true) that...* etc.

Here are a few examples:

Il est certain que...	Il est possible que... (s)
Il est vrai que...	Il est essentiel que... (s)
Il est évident que...	Il est naturel que... (s)

Avoir sa propre voiture, c'est formidable!

5.9 Adverbs

heureusement	évidemment
naturellement	**constamment**
attentivement	**de façon irresponsable**
doucement	

○ Adverbs describe how something is done: carefully, slowly, well.

○ Most adverbs are derived from the **feminine form of the adjective + -ment**. Look at these examples:

Masc. form	Fem. form	Adverb	
heureux	heureuse	**heureusement**	*happily*
naturel	naturelle	**naturellement**	*naturally*
général	générale	**généralement**	*generally*
lent	lente	**lentement**	*slowly*
doux	douce	**doucement**	*softly*
attentif	attentive	**attentivement**	*attentively*

○ There are some exceptions. If the adjective ends in a vowel, the adverb is derived from the masculine form. For example:

vrai	→	**vraiment**	*really*
absolu	→	**absolument**	*absolutely*
infini	→	**infiniment**	*infinitely*

○ Adjectives ending in **-ent** form their adverbs with **-emment**:

récent	→ **récemment**	*recently*
fréquent	→ **fréquemment**	*frequently*
évident	→ **évidemment**	*evidently*

The only exception to this rule is **lent**:

| lent | → **lentement** | *slowly* |

○ Adjectives ending in **-ant** form their adverbs with **-amment**:

| constant | → **constamment** | *constantly* |
| courant | → **couramment** | *fluently* |

○ A few common irregular adverbs need to be learned:

vite	*quickly*
bien	*well*
mal	*badly*
mieux	*better*
énormément	*greatly*
profondément	*deeply*
notamment	*notably; especially*

A〉〉 Newly qualified drivers don't always drive the way they've been taught to drive. Form adverbs from the adjectives below to fill the gaps in the text. The first letter of each missing adverb has been given.

doux	général	adroit
bon	constant	normal
dangereux	fréquent	attentif
absolu	lent	vrai
prudent	mauvais	

G_____ (**1**), les jeunes Français apprennent à conduire avec une auto-école. On leur conseille de conduire p_____ (**2**), de démarrer l_____ (**3**) et d'accélérer d_____ (**4**). N_____ (**5**), la plupart des jeunes écoutent a_____ (**6**) mais certains conduisent d_____ (**7**). F_____ (**8**) ils provoquent des accidents graves. Il est a_____ (**9**) essentiel que ces jeunes comprennent qu'ils sont v_____ (**10**) bêtes et dangereux. S'ils veulent b_____ (**11**) conduire, ils doivent surveiller c_____ (**12**) la façon dont ils conduisent. Il faut qu'ils comprennent qu'on admire davantage ceux qui conduisent a_____ (**13**) que ceux qui conduisent m_____ (**14**).

○ Note that adverbs can also be conveyed in a number of other ways:

   i.   **avec** + an abstract noun. For example:

avec tact	*tactfully*
avec enthousiasme	*enthusiastically*
avec méthode	*methodically*
avec entrain	*cheerfully*
avec impatience	*impatiently*
avec succès	*successfully*

○ Note that if the abstract noun is qualified by an adjective, **un** or **une** is used with the noun:

avec **un** plaisir évident	*with obvious pleasure*
avec **une** impatience grandissante	*with increasing impatience*

   ii.   By using one of the following phrases:

de façon + adjective
d'une façon + adjective
de manière + adjective
d'une manière + adjective

Le nombre de morts sur les routes a augmenté **de façon spectaculaire**.
The number of people killed on the roads has gone up dramatically.

L'État a répondu **de façon positive** aux problèmes de l'encombrement des routes françaises.
The State responded positively to the problems of overcrowding on French roads.

B» Use the nouns and adjectives given below to express these English adverbs.

1	angrily	**5**	lovingly
2	decisively	**6**	impressively
3	patiently	**7**	sympathetically
4	convincingly	**8**	efficiently

la sympathie	la patience	convaincant
la colère	efficace	impressionnant
l'amour	décisif	

5.10 The comparative and superlative of adverbs

Il faut conduire **plus lentement** et **moins agressivement**.
You must drive more slowly and less aggressively.

C'est Pierre qui conduit **le plus rapidement** mais c'est sa soeur qui conduit **le mieux**.
It's Pierre who drives the fastest but it's his sister who drives the best.

5.11 *Faire* + infinitive = to have something done

> si vous faites installer un lecteur de CD

O   Note the following example:

> J'ai **fait vérifier** les pneus.
> Literally this means: *I have made (someone) check the tyres.*
> In standard English we say: *I've had the tyres checked.*
> Similarly: *I have had the exhaust repaired.*
> J'ai **fait réparer** le tuyau d'échappement.

》 Imagine you've bought an old sports car. You've had lots of things done to it. Rephrase these sentences using **faire** + **infinitive** to convey what you had done e.g. On a vérifié la suspension. J'ai fait vérifier la suspension.

1.   On a changé les freins.
2.   On a remplacé les phares.
3.   On a réparé le toit.
4.   On a repeint la carrosserie.
5.   On a recouvert les sièges.
6.   On a installé un lecteur de CD.

5.12 Verbs + infinitive

> Il faut constamment faire attention.
> On doit apprendre à bien conduire.
> Sinon on risque de provoquer un grave accident.

○　Remember that when verbs are followed by an infinitive, some need **just the infinitive**, others need **de + infinitive**, and others need **à + infinitive**. Make a point of noting down from your reading and listening which construction particular verbs take when used with an infinitive. Look at these examples:

> **Il veut acheter** une voiture.
> *He wants to buy a car.*
>
> Elle a **décidé d'apprendre** à conduire.
> *She has decided to learn to drive.*
>
> Elle a **commencé à prendre** des leçons.
> *She has begun to have lessons.*

○　Look through the list below; then cover it up and test yourself by writing out the correct version of the sentences that follow.

devoir	– *to have to*
il vaut mieux	– *it is better to*
il faut	– *it is necessary to*
laisser quelqu'un faire…	– *to let someone do…*
savoir	– *to know how to*
aimer	– *to like to*
préférer	– *to prefer to*
apprendre à	– *to learn to*
continuer à	– *to continue to*
hésiter à	– *to hesitate to*
penser à	– *to think about doing…*
consister à	– *to consist in doing…*
commencer à	– *to begin to*
avoir tendance à	– *to tend to*
s'amuser à	– *to while away the time doing…*
contribuer à	– *to help to*
se préparer à	– *to prepare to*
essayer de	– *to try to*
éviter de	– *to avoid doing…*
manquer de	– *to fail to*
oublier de	– *to forget to*
il suffit de	– *it is enough to*
cesser de	– *to stop doing…*
il s'agit de	– *it is a question of doing…*
risquer de	– *to be liable to*
mériter de	– *to deserve to*

>> Complete what the instructor says by filling in the gaps with **à** or **de** where necessary.

1 Tu dois ___ faire attention tout le temps.
2 Il vaut mieux ___ démarrer lentement.
3 Apprends ___ utiliser ton rétroviseur tout le temps.
4 Continue ___ conduire comme ça une fois que tu auras le permis.
5 N'hésite pas ___ freiner tout de suite si tu vois des problèmes devant toi.
6 La bonne conduite consiste ___ savoir ___ s'adapter aux conditions changeantes.
7 Pense ___ changer de vitesse avant d'arriver au carrefour.
8 Il faut ___ commencer ___ penser aux problèmes comme si tu conduisais tout seul.
9 Essaie ___ être un conducteur responable.
10 Évite ___ conduire trop rapidement.
11 Ne manque pas ___ vérifier souvent ta vitesse.
12 N'oublie pas ___ regarder derrière toi avant d'ouvrir la portière.
13 Il ne suffit pas ___ conduire comme si tu étais tout seul sur la route.
14 Laisse ___ les autres ___ te dépasser s'ils le veulent.
15 Cesse ___ penser que tu es un pilote de course! Sinon tu risques ___ avoir un accident.
16 Il s'agit ___ arriver à sa destination sain et sauf.
17 Les jeunes ont tendance ___ conduire trop rapidement.

Now check your answers and learn the verbs you didn't get right.

6 Talking about people and things

Quelle bonne surprise! Quel plaisir de te retrouver ici!

Sophie is French and Julie is British. They worked together in Brussels for a time and now meet again by chance in Paris.

Sophie:	Julie! **Quelle bonne surprise! Quel plaisir de te retrouver** ici à Paris! Et tu as si **bonne** mine! **Tu es à Paris depuis longtemps**?	6.1 / 6.12 6.14
Julie:	**Depuis deux mois. J'ai essayé de te téléphoner** mais **on m'a dit** que tu avais déménagé.	6.3 / 6.6 6.3
Sophie:	Oui, c'est vrai. J'ai **un nouvel appartement** place d'Italie.	6.13
Julie:	**Le mien**, c'est **un bel appartement** à République que **mon amie Françoise m'a prêté**.	6.11 / 6.13 6.10 / 6.3
Sophie:	Alors tu es restée à Bruxelles combien de temps?	

Julie:	J'ai continué à travailler chez Unilever **pendant**	6.14
	six mois, puis je suis venue à Paris.	
Sophie:	Et que fais-tu à Paris?	
Julie:	**J'y travaille** comme secétaire et j'écris aussi	6.5 / 6.6
	des articles sur **le nouveau Paris**.	6.13
Sophie:	Et **tu vas y rester pour combien de temps**?	6.6 / 6.14
Julie:	**J'y reste** encore deux ou trois semaines. Je	6.5
	dois finir **mes articles** sur Paris	6.10
Sophie:	Et **ton travail** va bien?	6.10
Julie:	Oui. **Mon patron** est très exigeant sur le	6.10
	plan professionnel, mais **c'est un homme**	6.15
	sympathique. Je m'entends très bien **avec**	6.7
	lui et avec **sa femme** aussi. **Je les aime bien**.	6.10 / 6.2
	Ils m'invitent chez eux une fois par semaine	6.3 / 6.7
	parce qu'ils aiment parler anglais. **Leurs**	6.10
	enfants aussi. **Leur fille** est étudiante en droit	6.10
	et **leur fils** est très doué pour la musique. **Il**	6.10
	est très intéressant de leur parler en	6.6
	anglais... Tout va bien **pour toi** aussi?	6.7
Sophie:	Ah oui. **J'ai une bonne nouvelle à t'annoncer**.	6.12 / 6.9
	Je vais épouser Thomas Lemonnier. Tu	
	connais Thomas?	
Julie:	Bien sûr que **je le connais. C'est lui qui nous**	6.2 / 6.8
	a emmenées une fois à Ostende en voiture.	/ 6.6
	Dis-lui bonjour! Toutes **mes félicitations**!	6.6 / 6.10
	Je peux t'offrir quelque chose à boire?	6.6 / 6.9
Sophie:	C'est gentil. Mais je **dois te quitter** pour	6.6
	l'instant. **J'ai du travail à faire** cet après-midi.	6.9
	Mais on pourrait se revoir un soir.	
Julie:	**Quelle bonne idée... Donne-moi ton numéro**	6.1 / 6.12
	de téléphone. Alors vendredi soir peut-être,	/ 6.6
	si tu n'as **rien de spécial à faire**.	6.9

6.1 Expressing emotion using *quel*

> **Quelle bonne surprise!**
> **Quel plaisir de te retrouver à Paris!**

○ You are probably used to the word **quel**, as used in questions to translate *what* or *which*. Remember that it has to agree with the noun and has four forms, depending on whether the noun is masculine or feminine, singular or plural.

> **Quel** temps fait-il? (m.s.)
> *What's the weather like?*

> **Quelle** heure est-il? (f.s.)
> *What time is it?*

> **Quels** sports aimes-tu? (m.pl.)
> *What sports do you like?*

> **Quelles** matières préfères-tu? (f.pl.)
> *Which subjects do you prefer?*

○ These same words can be used in exclamations:

> **Quel** plaisir de te revoir!
> *What a treat to see you again!*

> **Quelle** coïncidence!
> *What a coincidence!*

> **Quels** beaux appartements!
> *What lovely flats!*

> **Quelles** belles photos!
> *What beautiful photos!*

○ Note that the French pattern is slightly different from the English:

Quel dommage!	*What **a** pity!*
Quelle catastrophe!	*What **a** disaster!*

A》 Give the French for the following exclamations.

1 What a good idea!
2 What a lovely surprise!
3 What a nice man!
4 What a lovely day!

B⟩⟩ Turn the following rather flat sentences into enthusiastic comments. Use **quel, quelle, quels**, or **quelles**, as appropriate.

1 C'est une bonne nouvelle.
2 C'est un enfant intelligent.
3 C'est une jolie robe.
4 C'est un bel appartement.
5 C'est un costume élégant.
6 C'est une belle ville.
7 Ce sont des filles charmantes.
8 Ce sont de beaux magasins.

6.2 Direct object pronouns: *le, la, les*

> **Tu connais Thomas? – Bien sûr que je le connais.**
> Tu aimes le travail de bureau? – Non, je le déteste!

○ **Le, la** and **les** are used as direct object pronouns, meaning *it, him, her* or *them*. Look at these examples:

i. When referring to things: **le/la = it, les = them**.
Tu aimes le rugby? *Do you like rugby?*
Non, je **le** déteste. *No, I hate it.*

Tu regardes souvent la télévision? *Do you watch television a lot?*
Oui, je **la** regarde tous les soirs. *Yes, I watch it every evening.*

Tu aimes les documentaires? *Do you like documentaries?*
Non, je ne **les** aime pas. *No, I don't like them.*

ii. When referring to people: **le** = *him*, **la** = *her*, **les** = *them*.

Pierre?...Je **le** rencontre quelquefois à la gare.
Pierre?...I sometimes meet him at the station.

Danièle?...Je **la** vois une fois par semaine.
Danièle?...I see her once a week.

Anne et Marc?...Je **les** connais assez bien.
Anne and Marc?...I know them fairly well.

○ Note that in French the pronoun comes before the verb, whereas in English the pronoun comes after the verb.

>> Sophie seems keen to learn all about Julie's life. Answer Sophie's questions for Julie, using a pronoun (**le, la** or **les**) to replace the underlined word.

1   – Tu vois souvent <u>tes parents</u>?
    – Non, je ___ vois tous les trois mois.

2   – Tu invites <u>tes amis</u> à dîner de temps en temps?
    – Je ___ invite très rarement.

3   – Tu connais <u>Françoise</u> depuis longtemps?
    – Non, je ___ connais depuis un an seulement.

4   - Tu vois souvent <u>François</u>?
    – Oui, je ___ vois presque tous les jours.

5   – Tu t'entends bien avec <u>la femme de ton patron</u>?
    – Oui, je ___ aime bien.

6   – Tu consultes <u>ton patron</u> au sujet des articles que tu écris?
    – Oui, je ___ consulte de temps en temps.

7   – Tu connais <u>Thomas</u> depuis combien de temps?
    – Je ___ connais depuis cinq ans.

8   – Tu aimes <u>les Français</u>?
    – Je crois plutôt que je ___ admire.

J'ai essayé de te parler!

6.3 Direct and indirect object pronouns: *me, te, nous, vous*

> **Ils m'invitent chez eux une fois par semaine.**
> **On m'a dit que tu avais déménagé.**

○ It is important to remember that

me	means	*me*	and	*to me,*
te	means	*you*	and	*to you,*
nous	means	*us*	and	*to us,*
vous	means	*you*	and	*to you.*

Here are some examples of the double use:

Mes amis **m'**invitent à passer la soirée chez eux.
My friends invite me to spend the evening with them.

Françoise **m'**a prêté son appartement.
Françoise has lent her flat to me.

Je suis content de **te** retrouver ici à Paris.
I'm pleased to see you again in Paris.

J'ai essayé de **te** parler.
I tried to speak to you.

○ Look at the following examples. Think of the two meanings of **me** and **te**.

Julie is talking about her boss:

Mon patron **me** connaît bien.
Il **me** comprend.
Il **me** parle souvent de son enfance à Paris.
Il **me** décrit les quartiers qu'il connaît bien.
Il **m'**encourage à finir mes articles sur Paris.

Julie is talking to Sophie about her boyfriend Thomas:

Il est évident que Thomas **t'**aime beaucoup.
Il **te** téléphone tous les soirs.
Il **te** donne des fleurs et des cadeaux de temps en temps.
Il **t'**invite à sortir presque tous les week-ends.
Il **t'**emmène souvent au cinéma ou au théâtre.
Tu as de la chance, toi!

>> Julie and Sophie are discussing going to the theatre. At the moment their conversation is incomplete. Add **me** and **te** so that it makes sense. Take special care with the position of **me** and **te**.

Julie: Thomas emmène souvent au théâtre?

Sophie: Oui, de temps en temps. Il contacte au cours de la journée pour voir si une pièce intéresse. Puis il vient chercher au bureau vers six heures.

Julie: On voit bien que Thomas gâte! Il doit aimer beaucoup!

Sophie: Et tes amis, ils ne invitent jamais à aller au théâtre?

Julie: Non, ils invitent à aller au cinéma ou au restaurant mais ils refusent de accompagner au théâtre. Ils demandent tout le temps pourquoi le théâtre intéresse et ils refusent de croire quand je dis qu'un vrai spectacle passionne beaucoup plus qu'un film.

Sophie: Alors moi, je invite à venir avec nous la prochaine fois. Thomas sera très content de emmener au théâtre, je le promets!

Dis-lui bonjour!

6.4 Indirect object pronouns: *lui* and *leur*

> Il est très intéressant de leur parler en anglais.
> Dis-lui bonjour!

O **lui** means *to him, to her*.
  leur means *to them*.

O Look at these examples:

> Je **lui** ai parlé hier soir.
> *I spoke to him/her last night.*

> Elle **leur** parle en anglais.
> *She speaks to them in English.*

A⟩⟩ Replace the underlined sections in the sentences below with the appropriate pronoun. Watch the position of the pronoun.

1 Je parle <u>aux jeunes</u> de toutes sortes de choses.
2 J'ai montré les articles <u>à mon patron</u>.
3 Je veux donner un cadeau <u>aux Ricard</u>.
4 Je vais téléphoner <u>à mes parents</u> ce soir.
5 Dis bonjour <u>à Thomas</u> de ma part!
6 Demande <u>à ton patron</u> de te donner un jour de congé!

O Be especially careful with sentences where the **to** idea is omitted in English. For example: *I sent **him** the photos* means *I sent the photos **to** him*. The French version must always be: Je **lui** ai envoyé les photos.

B⟩⟩ Translate these sentences into French.

1 I offered them the tickets.
2 I asked him to ring me.
3 I told them I was busy.
4 I gave her my telephone number.

6.5 *y* and *en*

> Tu travailles à Bruxelles?
> Oui, j'y travaille depuis 3 ans et je vais y rester.
> Tu as des amis là-bas?
> Oui, j'en ai beaucoup.

○ The pronoun **y** means *there* and is used to replace expressions containing à + place or en + country:

– Tu vas **au travail** en auto?
– J'**y** vais en métro.

○ The pronoun **en** means *some* or *of it/of them* and is used to replace expressions containing **du**, **de la**, **de l'**, **des** or just **de**, or nouns with a number or **beaucoup** (and similar structures):

– Tu as trouvé **du travail** facilement?
– Non, j'**en** ai cherché pendant près d'un mois.

》 The answers to the questions below are incomplete. Complete the answers by adding **y** or **en**, as appropriate.

1   Tu as écrit des articles sur Paris?
    Oui, j'ai écrit plusieurs.
2   Tu vas souvent au cinéma?
    Je vais deux fois par mois en moyenne.
3   Tu habites à Neuilly depuis longtemps?
    J'habite depuis deux mois seulement.
4   Ton patron a des enfants?
    Oui, il a deux.
5   Il y a combien d'employés dans le bureau?
    Il y a une dizaine.
6   Tu vas rester longtemps en France?
    Je vais rester encore plusieurs mois.
7   Tu vas écrire une série d'articles?
    J'espère écrire six.
8   Tu as passé combien de temps à Bruxelles?
    J'ai passé un an et demi.

6.6 Position of pronouns

> Elle m'a prêté son appartement.
> Je vais **lui** téléphoner.
> Dis-**lui** bonjour de ma part!
> Je **le leur** ai déjà expliqué.

○ Look at the position of the pronouns in these sentences:

> On **m'**a dit que tu avais déménagé.
> *They told me you had moved.*
>
> J'**y** travaille comme secrétaire.
> *I work there as a secretary.*
>
> Ils **m'**invitent chez eux une fois par semaine.
> *They invite me to their home once a week.*
>
> Bien sûr que je **le** connais.
> *Of course I know him.*
>
> Ils **nous** a emmenées à Ostende.
> *He took us to Ostende.*

Note that the pronouns come just before the verb in each case.

○ The above rule applies in all cases, except with positive commands, i.e. when you tell someone to do something. Pronouns then follow the verb. Look at these examples:

> Téléphone à tes parents ce soir!/Téléphone-**leur** ce soir!
> *Phone them this evening!*
>
> Dis à ton patron que tu as besoin de quelques jours de congé!/Dis-**lui** que tu as besoin de quelques jours de congé!
> *Tell him that you need a few days off!*
>
> Allez à l'agence demain!/Allez-**y** demain!
> *Go there tomorrow!*
>
> Montre-**nous** les articles!
> *Show us the articles!*

○ Note that **me** becomes **moi** and **te** becomes **toi** when used after a positive command. So *Give me your telephone number* is not Donne-**me** ton numéro de téléphone! but Donne-**moi** ton numéro de téléphone!

A⟩⟩ Rewrite the following sentences, replacing the underlined words with the appropriate pronouns and putting them in the correct place.

1 Je travaille <u>à Paris</u> comme secrétaire.
2 Invite <u>tes amis</u> à venir!
3 J'ai dit <u>au patron</u> que je serais un peu en retard.
4 Demande <u>à Thomas</u> de me téléphoner!
5 Je connais <u>Julie</u> depuis longtemps.
6 Regarde <u>ces articles</u>!
7 J'ai passé un an <u>à Bruxelles</u>.
8 Allons <u>au cinéma</u> vendredi soir!
9 Dis <u>aux jeunes</u> de parler français!
10 Habituellement, je parle <u>à leurs enfants</u> en anglais.

○ Sometimes there are two verbs, as in the following examples:

Tu **vas y rester** pour combien de temps?
Je **peux t'offrir** quelque chose à boire?
Je **dois te quitter** bientôt.
On **pourrait se revoir** un soir.

If there are two verbs, the pronoun goes immediately **before the infinitive**.

Je peux t'offrir quelque chose à boire?

B⟩⟩ Rephrase these sentences, using the correct form of **devoir** + **infinitive** instead of the imperative form.

1 Téléphone-lui ce soir! → Tu dois ___
2 Montre-leur ce que tu as écrit! → Tu dois ___
3 Explique-moi exactement ce que tu veux faire! → Tu dois ___
4 Demande-lui de te donner quelques jours de congé! → Tu dois ___
5 Donne-moi ta nouvelle adresse! → Tu dois ___
6 Dis-leur que tu veux rester à Paris! → Tu dois ___

○ Sometimes there is more than one pronoun in a sentence. Look at these examples:

– Il **te l'**a dit? *He told you so?*
– Oui, il **me l'**a dit hier soir. *Yes, he told me yesterday evening.*

– Il **vous l'**a dit? *He told you so?*
– Oui, il **nous l'**a dit hier soir. *Yes, he told us yesterday evening.*

– Je **le lui** ai expliqué. *I explained it to him.*
– Je **le leur** ai expliqué. *I explained it to them.*

– Combien d'élèves y a-t-il dans le groupe? *How many pupils are there in the group?*
– Il **y en** a 43. *There are 43.*

– Tu lui as donné des billets? *Have you given him some tickets?*
– Oui, je **lui en** ai donné cinq. *Yes, I've given him five.*

○ This table shows the sequence when two pronouns are used together:

1	2	3	4	5	6
me	le	lui	y	en	verb
te	la	leur			
se	les				
nous					
vous					
se					

C)) This dialogue took place when Sophie moved into her new flat. As it stands, it is incomplete. Complete what was said by placing the pronouns supplied in brackets in the correct order and position. (Don't forget that **me, te, le, la** change to **m', t', l'** before a vowel.)

Sophie:	Bonjour, madame. Les clefs de l'appartement de Mlle Prévost, vous pouvez donner (LES, ME)?
Concierge:	Les clefs? Je peux donner une (EN, VOUS), mais il a trois (EN, Y).
Sophie:	Vous devez donner au moins deux (ME, EN) puisque nous serons deux à y habiter.
Concierge:	Deux?
Sophie:	Mais oui, Mlle Prévost ne a pas dit (LE, VOUS)? Mon fiancé et moi. La deuxième clef, je vais donner (LUI, LA).
Concierge:	Alors je peux donner deux (VOUS, EN). Et le loyer, vous allez verser maintenant (LE, ME)?
Sophie:	Non. Mlle Prévost ne a pas dit (VOUS, LE)? Je vais envoyer le premier du mois (LE, LUI).
Concierge:	Ah bon.
Sophie:	Et les clefs, madame, vous allez chercher (LES, ME)? Je suis pressée.
Concierge:	Mais oui, madame. Tout de suite.

6.7 Pronouns used with prepositions (*chez moi, avec eux*)

chez moi	pour vous
chez nous	avec lui
pour toi	avec eux

○ Look at the use of pronouns used with prepositions in the following examples from the dialogue:

> Ils m'invitent **chez eux**.
> Je m'entends bien **avec lui**.
> Il est intéressant de parler **avec eux**.
> Tout va bien pour **toi aussi**?

O   Note that the pronouns **lui, eux, toi**, are used after a preposition.
    Other examples you may already know are with the preposition
    chez: chez moi, chez nous.

    The full list of these pronouns is as follows:

    moi   toi   lui   elle   nous   vous   eux   elles

    These pronouns can be used with prepositions like **avec** (*with*),
    chez (*at the house of*), **pour** (*for*), **après** (*after*), etc.

》   Rephrase what Julie says using the appropriate pronoun from the
    list above.

1   Je vais souvent à leur appartement.
    Je vais souvent chez ___.
2   Il vient souvent me rendre visite.
    Il vient souvent chez ___.
3   J'ai de bons rapports avec mon patron.
    Je m'entends bien avec ___.
4   Il nous a accompagnées à Ostende.
    Il est allé à Ostende avec ___.
5   J'aime beaucoup être en leur compagnie.
    J'aime beaucoup être avec ___.
6   On pourrait organiser une soirée dans ton appartement?
    On pourrait organiser une soirée chez ___.
7   Nous sortons ensemble quelquefois le soir, Sophie et moi.
    Je sors quelquefois le soir avec ___.
8   Je leur parle pendant des heures.
    Je passe beaucoup de temps à parler avec ___.

6.8 Pronouns used for emphasis

> **Tu as bonne mine, toi!**
> Et nous, qu'est-ce que nous allons faire?
> **C'est lui qui nous a emmenés à Ostende.**

O   The pronouns listed above are also used for emphasis.

> **Moi**, j'aime beaucoup la cuisine belge mais **lui**, il déteste les
> moules et les frites.
> *I love Belgian food be he hates mussels and chips.*

Tu as de la chance, **toi**. Tu habites en plein centre de Paris alors que **nous**, nous habitons dans un grand ensemble en banlieue.
You're lucky. You live right in the middle of Paris whereas we live on an estate in the suburbs.

>> Make these statements more emphatic.

1   J'aime beaucoup Paris mais il préfère Bruxelles.
2   Nous adorons le cinéma mais ils préfèrent le théâtre.
3   Je comprends assez bien l'anglais mais tu le parles très bien aussi.
4   Elle est toujours très chic mais j'aime porter des vêtements décontractés le weekend.
5   Tu veux toujours dîner au restaurant. Je préfère manger ici.
6   Nous utilisons le métro autant que possible mais ils vont partout en taxi.

6.9 Nouns + *à* + infinitive

J'ai des courses à faire après le travail mais ce soir je n'ai rien à faire.
Tu veux quelque chose à boire?

O   Look at these examples. What do they have in common?

J'ai une bonne nouvelle à annoncer.
I've got some good news to tell.

Je peux t'offrir quelque chose à boire?
can I get you something to drink?

Je n'ai rien à faire ce soir.
I've got nothing to do this evening.

Nouns or words like quelque chose, quelqu'un, (ne...) rien, (ne...) personne, beaucoup, trop are followed by **à** + *infinitive*.

》 Rephrase the following sentences so that they follow the pattern of the examples given above.

1 Je veux te dire quelque chose d'important.
J'ai ___
2 Je dois faire beaucoup de travail ce soir.
J'ai ___
3 Je dois préparer le dîner.
J'ai ___
4 On m'a demandé d'écrire des articles sur le nouveau Paris.
J'ai ___
5 Je dois interviewer deux personnes.
J'ai ___
6 Je suis libre vendredi soir.
Je n'ai rien ___ vendredi soir.
7 Tu veux boire quelque chose?
Tu veux ___?
8 Tu as faim?
Tu veux que je prépare ___?

6.10 Possessive adjectives

mon patron	notre compagnie
ma compagnie	nos clients
mes collègues	leur travail
mon expérience	leurs heures de travail

○ The French for *my* is **mon, ma** or **mes**:

My job is **mon emploi** (un emploi), *my company* is **ma compagnie** (une compagnie) and *my colleagues* is **mes collègues** (des collègues).

A》 Try these examples. Put the correct form **mon, ma** or **mes** with the words below.

1 le salaire
2 la feuille de paie
3 le compte en banque
4 les économies
5 la carte de crédit
6 le carnet de chèques
7 les dépenses
8 le portefeuille

○ The French for *your* is **ton, ta** or **tes**; **his, her** or *its* is **son, sa** or **ses**. Look at these examples:

ton emploi	*your job*	**son** salaire	*his/her salary*
ta ville	*your town*	**sa** maison	*his/her house*
tes collègues	*your colleagues*	**ses** enfants	*his/her children*

○ Note that with feminine words beginning with a **vowel (or mute h)** e.g. une amie, une adresse, une école, une équipe, une auto, une histoire, **mon** has to be used instead of **ma**. This is to avoid the sound gap there would otherwise be, between **ma** and the vowel which follows. For example:

my car is not ma auto but **mon auto**
my friend Françoise is not ma amie Françoise but **mon amie** Françoise.

Similarly, **son** is used instead of **sa** and **ton** is used instead of **ta**.

his/her school is not sa école but **son** école
your address is not ta adresse but **ton** adresse

B》 Fill in the gaps with the correct form of **mon, ma** or **mes** to complete what Julie says about her job interview in Paris. Use the information given in this box to help you.

un entretien	une enfance	une éducation
des études	une attitude	une expérience
des connaissances	une opinion	un emploi
des ambitions	une écriture	

_____ **(1)** entretien? Ça s'est très bien passé. D'abord, on m'a posé beaucoup de questions sur _____ **(2)** enfance et sur _____ **(3)** éducation, sur _____ **(4)** études et sur _____ **(5)** attitude vis-à-vis du monde du travail. J'ai parlé de _____ **(6)** expérience chez Unilever et de _____ **(7)** connaissances en matière d'informatique. On m'a demandé _____ **(8)** opinion sur _____ **(9)** emploi à Bruxelles. Enfin, j'ai parlé de _____ **(10)** ambitions pour l'avenir. J'ai fait bonne impression, je crois. C'est seulement _____ **(11)** écriture qu'ils ont critiquée.

C》 Julie finds that suburban life is not as bad as she thought. Complete the text below with **son, sa** or **ses**. Use the information given in the box to help you.

une arrivée	un lieu de travail	une amie	un appartement

Avant _____ **(1)** arrivée à Paris, _____ **(2)** expérience de la vie de banlieue était limitée. À Bruxelles, elle habitait à proximité de _____ **(3)** lieu de travail et _____ **(4)** opinion était que la vie de banlieue était insupportable. Mais à Paris, _____ **(5)** amis et _____ **(6)** collègues lui ont expliqué les problèmes du logement et _____ **(7)** attitude a dû changer. Et maintenant qu'elle habite dans l'appartement que _____ **(8)** amie Françoise lui a prêté, _____ **(9)** opinion sur la vie de banlieue est tout à fait différente. _____ **(10)** nouvel apartement lui plaît beaucoup, _____ **(11)** voisins de palier sont très aimables et elle peut sortir avec _____ **(12)** amis le soir et rentrer chez elle sans difficulté.

○ The word for *our* in French is **notre** or **nos**; and *your* is **votre** or **vos**:

notre compagnie	*our company*
nos clients	*our clients*
votre patron	*your boss*
vos collègues	*your colleagues*

Use **notre/votre** if the noun is singular, and **nos/vos** if the noun is plural.

D>> Use the correct form, **notre, nos, votre** or **vos** to complete the following dialogue in which Julie talks to her boss and his wife about learning English.

Julie:	J'ai l'impression que _____ **(1)** enfants aiment parler anglais.
M. Ricard:	Oui, nous avons toujours encouragé _____ **(2)** enfants à apprendre les langues. _____ **(3)** parents à nous n'avaient pas les moyens de nous envoyer à l'étranger et _____ **(4)** éducation en a beaucoup souffert. Alors nous avons tout fait pour que _____ **(5)** enfants puissent bénéficier de cette expérience.
Julie:	Et _____ **(6)** enfants aiment la Grande-Bretagne?
Mme Ricard:	Oui, beaucoup. Ils sont toujours allés chez _____ **(7)** amis anglais où ils ont été très bien accueillis.
Julie:	Et il me semble que _____ **(8)** maison est toujours ouverte à _____ **(9)** amis anglais.
M. Ricard	Nous sommes toujours prêts à accueillir _____ **(10)** amis anglais. Comme ça, nous perfectionnons _____ **(11)** connaissances de l'anglais et nous donnons aussi à _____ **(12)** enfants l'occasion de parler anglais.

○ Look at the following examples from the dialogue:

leur fils   **leur** fille   **leurs** enfants

You can see that there are only two ways of expressing the English idea of **their: leur** + singular noun and **leurs** + plural noun.

○ Remember that **ses** never means *their*: **ses enfants** can mean only *his children* or *her children*.

E>> Use **leur** or **leurs** to complete what Julie says about her boss and his family.

Sa femme et lui aiment que _____ **(1)** enfants viennent passer la soirée chez eux. _____ **(2)** fils s'exprime bien en anglais mais _____ **(3)** fille est plus timide. Ils parlent de _____ **(4)** études et de _____ **(5)** copains et ils donnent _____ **(6)** opinions sur tous les sujets d'actualité. _____ **(7)** mère les écoute attentivement et semble partager _____ **(8)** idées, mais _____ **(9)** père au contraire n'accepte pas si facilement _____ **(10)** affirmations et il critique souvent _____ **(11)** point de vue. Moi, je corrige quelquefois _____ **(12)** erreurs mais _____ **(13)** anglais est assez correct et la plupart du temps, je me contente d'écouter _____ **(14)** conversation.

○ **leur** or **leurs**? In English we tend to say: *"A lot of women go out to work instead of staying at home and only looking after their husbands and families."*
The French, on the other hand, presume that each of the women has only one husband and one family. The French usage therefore tends to be: "Beaucoup de femmes travaillent à l'extérieur au lieu de rester à la maison pour s'occuper exclusivement de leur mari et de leur famille."

F⟩⟩ Translate these sentences into French.

1 Many Parisians leave their cars in the street.
2 A lot of Frenchmen like their wives to be at home when they come in! (Beaucoup de Français aiment que ___ soit à la maison quand ils rentrent!)
3 A lot of children make their beds in order to help their parents.
4 Very few people have time to tidy their houses before they go out in the morning.

6.11 Possessive pronouns

J'ai un nouvel appartement place d'Italie – Le mien, c'est un bel appartement à République.

○ Possessive pronouns, such as **le mien, le tien, le sien, le nôtre, le leur** are used to convey the idea of *mine, yours, his, hers, ours, theirs*.

Note that there are four words for *mine*:

masculine singular	le mien
feminine singular	la mienne
masculine plural	les miens
feminine plural	les miennes

○ Study carefully the examples below.

J'ai un appartement place d'Italie. – **Le mien**, c'est à République.
Ta compagnie est plus dynamique que **la mienne**.
Tes collègues semblent plus aimables que **les miens**.
Tes conditions de travail sont plus agréables que **les miennes**.

Similarly yours: **le tien la tienne les tiens les tiennes**
his/hers: **le sien la sienne les siens les siennes**

○ Note that there are only three variations for **ours, yours, theirs**:

masculine singular	**le nôtre**	**le vôtre**	**le leur**
feminine singular	**la nôtre**	**la vôtre**	**la leur**
plural	**les nôtres**	**les vôtres**	**les leurs**

≫ Replace the underlined words with the relevant possessive pronouns.

1 Ton immeuble est plus prestigieux que <u>notre immeuble</u>.
2 Ta compagnie paie mieux que <u>ma compagnie</u>.
3 Mon appartement est plus petit que <u>votre appartement</u>.
4 Mais votre appartement est plus près du centre que <u>mon appartement</u>.
5 Je crois que nos produits sont meilleurs que <u>leurs produits</u>.
6 Mes collègues sont plus ouverts que <u>tes collègues</u>.
7 Notre compagnie est plus dynamique que <u>leur compagnie</u>.
8 Thomas pense que mon ordinateur est moins efficace que <u>son ordinateur</u>.

6.12 Agreement of adjectives

Bonjour	Une bonne nouvellee
Quel plaisir!e	Quelle bonne idée!
le nouveau Paris	un nouvel appartement

○ Most adjectives follow the same pattern. For example:

masculine singular: grand   feminine singular: grand**e**
masculine plural: grand**s**   feminine plural: grand**es**

○ There are several exceptions. Adjectives ending in **-e** in the masculine singular are the same in the feminine singular. The masculine and feminine plurals are the same. For example:

Il est **malade**.   Elle est **malade** aussi.
Ils sont **malades**.   Elles sont **malades** aussi.

○ Adjectives ending in **-s** and **-x** are the same in the masculine singular and plural:

> Il est **gros**.　　　　Ils sont **gros**.
> Il est **heureux**.　　　Ils sont **heureux**.

○ A number of adjectives have irregular feminine forms. Several of them require a doubling of the consonant:

Masculine form	Feminine form	Similar adjectives
bon	bonne	mignon, mignonne
gentil	gentille	pareil, pareille
naturel	naturelle	adjectives ending in -el e.g. essentiel, essentielle traditionnel, traditionnelle, tel, telle
net	nette	muet, muette
moyen	moyenne	adjectives ending in -en e.g. ancien, ancienne européen, européenne quotidien, quotidienne
gros	grosse	gras, grasse bas, basse épais, épaisse

○ Adjectives ending in **-er** change to **-ère** in the feminine:

> cher, chère　　　premier, première　　　dernier, dernière

○ Adjectives ending in -**f** change to -**ve** in the feminine:

> actif, active　　　vif, vive
> sportif, sportive　　neuf, neuve

○ Adjectives ending in -**eux** change to -**euse** in the feminine:

> heureux, heureuse　　dangereux, dangereuse
> luxueux, luxueuse

○ Adjectives ending in **-et** change to -**ète** in the feminine:

> inquiet, inquiète   secret, secrète
> discrèt, discrète   complet, complète

○ The following adjectives do not fall into a fixed pattern:

Masculine form	Feminine form	Similar adjectives
blanc	blanche	franc, franche
frais	fraîche	
long	longue	
sec	sèche	
public	publique	
beau	belle	nouveau, nouvelle
vieux	vieille	
faux	fausse	
doux	douce	
fou	folle	mou, molle
favori	favorite	

○ Note these irregular masculine plural forms:

> **beau** becomes **beaux**
> **nouveau** become **nouveaux**

○ Most adjectives ending in **-al** change to **-aux** in the plural:

> social, sociaux   amical, amicaux
> national, nationaux   principal, principaux

》 Look carefully at the irregular feminine forms noted above. Then make the adjectives in brackets agree with the nouns they describe.

Nicole est une (VIEUX **1**) amie. C'est en fait une (ANCIEN **2**) élève de mon collège. Elle a toujours été très (GENTIL **3**) avec moi et au fond c'est une femme très (DOUX **4**). Mais depuis qu'elle travaille à Paris, elle mène une vie (PROFESSIONNEL **5**) très (ACTIF **6**) et elle est devenue plus (AGRESSIF **7**). Elle parle d'une voix plus (SEC **8**)

qu'avant. Cela peut donner une (FAUX **9**) impression de sa
personnalité. Il y a deux ans, sa mère est morte après une (LONG **10**)
maladie et cela l'a rendue très (MALHEUREUX **11**). Quand je l'ai vue
l'année (DERNIER **12**), elle paraissait presque (VIEUX **13**). Elle qui
était assez (SPORTIF **14**), elle est devenue (GROS **15**). Elle travaille
de (LONG **16**) heures au bureau et elle semble (INQUIET **17**) tout le
temps. La vie qu'elle mène me semble peu (NATUREL **18**) et même
un peu (FOU **19**). Je crois qu'une (NOUVEAU **20**) vie plus
(ACTIF **21**) sur le plan social est (ESSENTIEL **22**) si elle veut
retrouver son (ANCIEN **23**) verve.

6.13 The irregular adjectives: *beau, nouveau, vieux*

un beau site	un bel appartement
un nouveau quartier	un nouvel appartement
un vieux village	un vieil hôtel

O   The adjectives **beau** (beautiful), **nouveau** (new) and **vieux** (old)
have the following forms:

un **beau** quartier	une **belle** ville
de **beaux** immeubles	de **belles** places
un **nouveau** centre	une **nouvelle** piscine
de **nouveaux** équipements	de **nouvelles** maisons
un **vieux** village	une **vieille** église
de **vieux** bâtiments	de **vieilles** rues

O   These three adjectives have a special form used only with nouns in
the **masculine singular** beginning with a **vowel** or a mute **h**.
This is to avoid the sound gap that would otherwise occur.
So instead of un beau hôtel it is un **bel hôtel**. Instead of un
nouveau emploi it is un **nouvel emploi**. Instead of un vieux ami it
is un **vieil ami**.

○ Note that there is no problem with feminine words beginning with a vowel. There is no sound gap to cause problems. The following are correct: **une belle église, une nouvelle auto, une vieille école**

Alors, tu as un nouvel emploi?

》 Supply the correct form of **beau**, **nouveau** or **vieux** to complete this conversation between Sophie and Julie.

Julie: Tu voudrais habiter une (NOUVEAU **1**) maison en banlieue?

Sophie: Mais non, je préfère mon (NOUVEAU **2**) immeuble au centre de Paris. Alors, tu habites un (BEAU **3**) appartement à République? C'est dans un (NOUVEAU **4**) immeuble?

> *Julie*: Non, c'est un (VIEUX **5**) immeuble. J'aime beaucoup le (VIEUX **6**) quartier où j'habite. Il y a de (BEAU VIEUX **7**) magasins et de (VIEUX **8**) rues. Je déteste les (BEAU **9**) places et les (NOUVEAU **10**) immeubles modernes qu'on construit un peu partout à Paris... Alors, tu as un (NOUVEAU **11**) emploi?
>
> *Sophie*: Oui, dans une (NOUVEAU **12**) entreprise d'informatique.

6.14 How to translate *for* with expressions of time (*depuis, pendant, pour*)

> Tu travailles à Paris depuis longtemps?
> J'ai travaillé là pendant six mois.
> Tu vas rester à Paris pour combien de temps?

○ **Pendant** is usually used to translate *for* meaning *time during which*:

Julie a travaillé à Bruxelles **pendant** un an.

Pendant is used with a past tense for completed actions, i.e. *Julie worked in Brussels for a year, then she came to Paris.*

○ **Depuis** is used when the action described is still going on:

Julie travaille à Paris **depuis** deux mois.

The situation has started in the past and is still going on. Julie has been working in Paris over the last couple of months and is still working there. This is why the French use a present tense with **depuis**.

○ **Pour** is used only when the period of time is later on in the future:

Julie va rester à Paris **pour** deux ou trois semaines.
Julie is going to stay on in Paris for two or three weeks.

129

A›› Choose between **pendant, depuis** and **pour** to complete these sentences correctly.

Julie et Sophie se connaissent _____ **(1)** longtemps.
Elles ont travaillé ensemble _____ **(2)** neuf mois à Bruxelles.
Sophie aime son nouvel appartement: elle y habite _____ **(3)** un mois seulement.
Thomas et Sophie ont vécu ensemble _____ **(4)** deux ans, puis Sophie est allée travailler à Bruxelles.
Thomas est toujours à l'université: il fait des études de médecine _____ **(5)** cinq ans. Après cela, il va travailler dans un hôpital _____ **(6)** deux ans. Avant d'aller à l'université, il a fait son service militaire _____ **(7)** un an.
Après leur mariage, Sophie et Thomas vont continuer à habiter Paris _____ **(8)** deux ou trois ans.

B›› **Depuis** needs particular attention. What will the form of the verb be in the following sentences?

1 Julie (CONNAÎTRE) Sophie depuis bientôt deux ans.
2 Elle (ÊTRE) à Paris depuis deux mois.
3 Elle (TRAVAILLER) pour M. Ricard depuis six semaines.
4 Elle (HABITER) chez Françoise depuis deux mois.
5 Elle (ÉTUDIER) le français depuis longtemps.
6 Elle (APPRENDRE) l'italien depuis plus d'un an.

C›› Translate the above sentences into English.

6.15 Using *c'est* and *ce sont* with things and people

C'est une compagnie prestigieuse.
C'est un homme sympathique.
Ce sont des contrats très importants.
Ce sont des collègues très aimables.

○ The use of **c'est** and **ce sont** seems natural when applied to things. For example:

C'est une école mixte.	*It's a mixed school.*
Ce sont des bureaux très chic.	*They are very smart offices.*

○ The same construction, however, can be used for talking about people:

C'est un garçon sérieux.	*He's a serious boy.*
C'est une jolie fille.	*She's a pretty girl.*
Ce sont des parents très gentils.	*They are very kind parents.*
Ce sont de bons amis	*They are good friends.*

○ Note that when using the plural version, it is either ce sont **de**... or ce sont **des**..., depending on the position of the adjective.

≫ Rephrase these sentences using **c'est un**... or **c'est une**...

1 Cette fille est très sportive.
2 Ce garçon est très intelligent.
3 Cet homme est travailleur.
4 Cette femme est très énergique.

7 Expressing choice and preference

Mme Hénin manages to find a flat in the inner suburbs of Paris with the help of a sympathetic estate agent.

At the estate agent's...

Mme Hénin:	Je cherche un appartement à louer dans **ce**	7.6
	quartier. Naturellement, **je préférerais**	7.4
	quelque chose de **pas trop cher**.	7.3
Agent:	J'ai exactement ce que vous cherchez,	
	madame.Voici les plans de deux appartements...	
	Lequel préférez-vous? **Celui-ci est un peu**	7.8 / 7.7
	plus grand mais il est au cinquième étage et	
	il n'y a pas d'ascenseur.	7.1
Mme Hénin:	**Et celui-là?**	7.7
Agent:	**Celui-là est au troisième**. **Cet appartement**	7.7 / 7.6
	n'est pas cher, 4000 francs par mois	
	seulement.	
Mme Hénin:	4000 francs! **On n'est pas assez riche pour**	7.3
	payer un tel loyer. **Si on avait autant**	7.5
	d'argent, on pourrait louer un appartement	7.4
	en plein centre!	
Agent:	Puisque vous travaillez dans Paris, **cet**	7.6
	appartement serait idéal pour vous. Il y a	7.4
	plusieurs stations de métro à proximité.	7.2
Mme Hénin:	Mais **on ne pourrait jamais** payer un tel	7.4
	loyer.	
Agent:	**Je pourrais** demander au propriétaire **s'il**	7.4
	serait prêt à accepter un rabais. On a eu	
	tant de problèmes avec les derniers locataires.	7.1
	Quand ils ont quitté l'appartement, il y avait	
	énormément de dégâts. Il y avait **de la**	7.1
	peinture sur le plancher, il y avait **des taches**	7.1
	de vin rouge sur les murs et **de l'eau** partout	7.1
	dans la salle de bains.	

Mme Hénin:	Moi, **je serais très contente de louer**	7.4
	l'appartement si le loyer était moins élevé...	7.5

In the flat...

M. Hénin:	Que penses-tu de **cet appartement**?	7.6
Mme Hénin:	**Je préférerais celui de la rue de Fontenay,**	7.4 / 7.7
	celui que nous avons visité hier soir.	7.7
M. Hénin:	Ah oui, **celui qui donnait sur le bois** de	7.7
	Vincennes.	
Mme Hénin:	Oui, **celui-là m'a beaucoup plu** mais le loyer	7.7
	était beaucoup trop élevé. J'aime bien	7.3
	celui-ci.	7.7
M. Hénin:	Bon, je crois **qu'on ne trouverait rien** de	7.4
	mieux à ce prix. Téléphonons à l'agence tout	
	de suite.	

7.1 Expressions of quantity and negatives + *de*

> tant de problèmes
> beaucoup de dégâts
> Il n'y a pas d'ascenseur.

○ You are probably aware of the following patterns:

le vin	→ **du** vin	*some wine*
la bière	→ **de la** bière	*some beer*
l'eau	→ **de l'**eau	*some water*
les bouteilles	→ **des** bouteilles	*some bottles*

○ It is, however, still difficult when in English the word *some* is left out. How would you translate the following sentence?

> "*With their pocket-money young people buy records, clothes and drinks.*"

You might say:

> "Avec leur argent de poche, les jeunes achètent **les** disques, **les** vêtements et **les** boissons."

This means that each young person buys specific records, clothes and drinks or all the records, clothes and drinks that are available, which is not the case. Each person only buys a certain number of records, clothes and drinks. The sentence should read:

> "Avec leur argent de poche, les jeunes achètent **des** disques, **des** vêtements et **des** boissons."

○ There are two occasions when **du, de la, de l'** and **des** are replaced by **de**:

i. After words like **beaucoup** (beaucoup de problèmes, beaucoup de bruit). The main expressions of quantity which follow the same pattern as **beaucoup** are:

plus de (*more*)
moins de (*less*)
trop de (*too many*)
assez de (*enough*)

tant de *(so much, so many)*
autant de *(as much, as many)*
un peu de *(a little)*
peu de *(very little)*
pas mal de *(quite a lot of)*
un tas de *(plenty of)*
énormément de *(a great deal of)*

la plupart *(most)* does not follow this rule:

Most of the tenants is **la plupart des** locataires.

Most of the time is **la plupart du** temps.

ii.   After a negative **du, de la, de l', des, un** and **une** are also
        replaced by **de**:

– Il y a un concierge dans l'immeuble?
Is there a caretaker in the block of flats?

–Non, il n'y a pas **de** concierge.
No, there isn't a caretaker.

– Il y a des chiens dans l'immeuble?
Are there any dogs in the block of flats?

– Non, il n'y a pas **de** chiens.
No, there aren't any dogs.

O   Be especially careful with words beginning with a vowel. Don't
     make the mistake of using **d'argent** to mean *some money*. The
     correct form is **de l'argent**.

This full form must be used in all circumstances except, as is noted
above, when

i.   there is an expression of quantity:

Ils ont **beaucoup d'argent**.
They have a lot of money.

ii.   it is used with a negative:

Je n'ai plus d'argent.
I have no more money.

A⟩⟩ Complete what this caretaker has to say to a new tenant. Use **du, de la, de l', des, d'** or **de** as appropriate.

Les derniers locataires ont causé énormément _____ (**1**) problèmes. Ils faisaient trop _____ (**2**) bruit, ils faisaient _____ (**3**) bruit tout le temps. La plupart _____ (**4**) temps, il y avait trop _____ (**5**) monde dans l'appartement. Ils faisaient tant _____ (**6**) bruit que personne ne pouvait dormir. La plupart _____ (**7**) locataires sont assez âgés et ils voulaient plus _____ (**8**) calme. Les derniers locataires buvaient _____ (**9**) bière aussi. Le matin, dans l'escalier, il y avait toujours beaucoup _____ (**10**) canettes de bière. J'espère bien que vous ferez moins _____ (**11**) bruit et que vous aurez plus _____ (**12**) respect pour les autres locataires.

B⟩⟩ The estate agent is showing Mme Hénin around a flat. Complete the dialogue by filling in the gaps with **un, une, du, de la, de l', des, de,** or **d'**, as appropriate.

Mme Hénin: Il y a _____ (**1**) locataires au-dessus de nous?
Agent: Non, il n'y a pas _____ (**2**) locataires au cinquième.
Mme Hénin: Nous avons _____ (**3**) voiture. Est-ce qu'il y a _____ (**4**) parking?
Agent: Non, il n'y a pas _____ (**5**) parking.
Mme Hénin: Il y a _____ (**6**) ascenseur dans l'immeuble?
Agent: Non, il n'y a pas _____ (**7**) ascenseur non plus.
Mme Hénin: On emploie _____ (**8**) concierge?
Agent: Non, on n'emploie pas _____ (**9**) concierge. On n'a jamais eu _____ (**10**) concierge.
Mme Hénin: Et les poubelles? Il y a toujours _____ (**11**) poubelles dans l'entrée?
Agent: Pas de problème, madame. On ne laisse jamais _____ (**12**) poubelles dans l'entrée. Il y a _____ (**13**) vide-ordures à chaque étage.
Mme Hénin: Il y a d'autres appartements à louer dans ce quartier? Je cherche _____ (**14**) appartement pas trop cher.
Agent: Il y a _____ (**15**) appartements, madame, mais il n'y a pas _____ (**16**) appartements à prix modeste.

7.2 How to translate *a few, several, some*

quelques magasins
plusieurs stations de métro
certains immeubles

○ There are some adjectives indicating number or quantity that need to be learned: **quelques** *(a few)*, **plusieurs** *(several)*, **certains** *(some)*. Since they are adjectives, they do not require **de**:

> Nous pourrons inviter **quelques amis** à dîner.
> *We will be able to invite a few friends to dinner.*

> Il y a **plusieurs appartements** à vendre.
> *There are several flats for sale.*

> **Certains locataires** font beaucoup de bruit; d'autres sont plus calmes.
> *Some tenants make a lot of noise; others are quieter.*

○ Watch out for this use of **certains** meaning *some* as opposed to *others*. **Quelques** cannot be used in this sense. **Quelques** means *a few*.

Certains locataires font beaucoup de bruit.

○ If you want to express the idea of *a few* when there is no noun to
follow, use **quelques-uns** or **quelques-unes**:

> La plupart des appartements ont été vendus mais il y a
> **quelques appartements** qui sont toujours à vendre.
> *Most of the flats have been sold but there are still a few flats for sale.*

La plupart des appartements ont été vendus mais il y en a
quelques-uns qui sont toujours à vendre.
Most of the flats have been sold but there are still a few for sale.

》 Complete the gaps in this text, using **quelques, quelques-uns,
quelques-unes, plusieurs, certain(e)s, la plupart** or **beaucoup**, as
appropriate. (Very occasionally, more than one will fit.)

_____ (1) des locataires dans cet immeuble sont des gens
convenables mais il y en a _____ (2) (cinq ou six ménages en tout)
qui causent _____ (3) de problèmes. _____ (4) font du bruit,
d'autres invitent _____ (5) d'amis et semblent parler très fort
_____ (6) du temps. _____ (7) familles (deux ou trois peut-être) se
disputent à tue-tête _____ (8) fois par semaine. _____ (9) soirs, ça
continue pendant _____ (10) heures. Mais comme j'ai déjà dit,
_____ (10) des locataires ne dérangent personne. _____ (12)
locataires ne vous disent même pas bonjour mais d'autres s'arrêtent
pour vous parler un peu. _____ (13) du temps, on n'a pas
_____ (14) de choses à se dire mais du moins on fait un effort.

7.3 *Trop* and *assez*

> **On n'est pas assez riche pour payer un tel loyer.**
> **Nous sommes trop pauvres pour acheter une maison en banlieue.**

○ **Trop** *(too)* and **assez** *(enough)* take similar constructions:

i. With an adjective:

> L'appartement est **trop** cher.
> *the flat is too expensive.*

> Cette chambre est **assez** grande pour les deux enfants.
> *This room is big enough for the two children.*

ii. With a noun:

Les locataires faisaient **trop de** bruit.
The tenants made too much noise.

Nous n'avons pas **assez de** place.
We don't have enough room.

iii. With an infinitive:

Cette pièce est **trop petite pour** servir de salle de séjour.
This room is too small to be used as the living room.

Nous ne sommes pas **assez riches pour** louer un appartement en plein centre.
We aren't rich enough to rent a flat right in the centre.

>> Complete the rephrased sentences below, using **trop** or **assez...
pour + infinitive**, as appropriate.

1 Nous n'avons pas le temps de repeindre l'appartement.
   Nous avons trop de travail ___

2 Les enfants sont trop jeunes: ils ne peuvent pas aller à l'école tout seuls.
   Les enfants sont trop ___

3 Les magasins sont trop loin de chez nous. Nous ne pouvons pas y aller à pied.
   Nous sommes trop loin des magasins ___

4 Nous n'avons pas le moyens de louer un appartement dans Paris.
   Nous n'avons pas assez ___

5 Nous n'allons jamais à Paris le soir. C'est trop loin.
   Nous habitons trop loin de Paris ___

6 Acheter une maison en banlieue? Nous ne sommes pas si riches que ça!
   Nous ne sommes pas assez ___

7.4 The conditional tense

> **je préférerais**
> **je serais**
> **je pourrais**

○ You have probably already come across the conditional tense of the verb **vouloir**: **je voudrais** (*I would like*). Similarly, **j'habiterais** means *I would live*, and **j'achèterais** means *I would buy*.

○ To form the conditional tense, you need the **future stem of the verb + imperfect endings**. Look at this example with the verb **aimer**:

j'**aimerais**	*I would like*
tu **aimerais**	*you would like*
il/elle/on **aimerai**t	*he/she/one would like*
nous **aimerions**	*we would like*
vous **aimeriez**	*you would like*
ils/elles **aimeraient**	*they would like*

○ There is only one set of endings, but there are some important irregular verbs you need to learn thoroughly. The stem used in the conditional tense is the same as the stem used in the future tense:

acheter	*to buy*	j'achèterais
aller	*to go*	j'irais
appeler	*to call*	j'appellerais
avoir	*to have*	j'aurais
devoir	*to have to*	je devrais
envoyer	*to send*	j'enverrais
être	*to be*	je serais
faire	*to do/make*	je ferais
jeter	*to throw*	je jetterais
se lever	*to get up*	je me lèverais
pouvoir	*to be able to*	je pourrais
savoir	*to know*	je saurais
venir	*to come*	je viendrais
voir	*to see*	je verrais
vouloir	*to want*	je voudrais

○ Note also the following useful examples:

| il faut | → | il faudrait | *it would be necessary* |
| il vaut mieux | → | il vaudrait mieux | *it would be better* |

》 Mme Hénin would like to leave her small flat in central Paris and take her three children to live in the suburbs. She thinks about what her life would be like. Put the verbs in brackets into the conditional tense to complete what she says.

1 J'(HABITER) en banlieue.
2 J'(ACHETER) une petite voiture.
3 J'(APPRENDRE) à conduire.
4 Je (SORTIR) beaucoup plus le week-end.
5 Je (PROFITER) du soleil et du plein air.
6 Je (FAIRE) des promenades avec les enfants tous les jours.
7 Je ne (DEVOIR) pas surveiller les enfants tout le temps.
8 Je (POUVOIR) les laisser jouer dehors.
9 J'(ALLER) à la piscine avec les enfants.
10 Je (VOIR) mes voisines plus souvent.
11 J'(AVOIR) un bel appartement.
12 Je (ÊTRE) beaucoup plus heureuse.

Je ne sais pas si je voudrais vivre ici!

7.5 *Si* clauses

si le loyer était moins élevé

O In the following example, **si** means *if* in the sense of *provided that*:

> Nous louerons cet appartement **si** le loyer n'est pas trop élevé.
> *We'll rent the flat if (provided that) the rent is not too high.*

O When using **si**, these rules about which tenses to use have to be followed:

i. **si + *present tense* + *future tense*:**

> **Si je loue** (PRESENT) cet appartement, **je pourrai** (FUTURE) arriver au bureau en 20 minutes.
> *If I rent this flat, I'll be able to get to work in 20 minutes.*

Si j'avais plus d'argent...

ii.　**si** + *imperfect tense* + *conditional tense*:

Si j'avais (IMPERFECT) plus d'argent, **j'achèterais**
(CONDITIONAL) un appartement en banlieue.
If I had more money, I would buy a flat in the suburbs.

iii.　**si** + *pluperfect tense* + *conditional perfect tense*:

The conditional perfect is made up of *the conditional tense
of the auxiliary verb* + *the past participle*

Si j'avais su (PLUPERFECT) que les appartements seraient
si chers à Paris, **j'aurais refusé** (CONDITIONAL PERFECT)
la mutation.
*If I had known that flats in Paris were going to be so expensive, I
would have refused to change jobs.*

○　Take special care to distinguish between the future and conditional
endings, as they are so similar. Look at these examples with the
verb **louer** (to hire):

future	conditional
je louerai	je louerais
tu loueras	tu louerais
il/elle louera	il/elle louerait
nous louerons	nous louerions
vous louerez	vous loueriez
ils/elles loueront	ils/elles loueraient

A⟩⟩ Complete these sentences by putting the verb in brackets into the
correct tense. Remember to check carefully the tense of the verb
in the main clause.

1　Si je (TRAVAILLER) à Paris, j'habiterais dans la banlieue proche.
2　Si nous (LOUER) cet appartement, nous aurons beaucoup plus
　de place.
3　Si les enfants (AVOIR) une grande chambre, ils pourraient y
　faire leurs devoirs.
4　Je n'hésiterais pas à choisir cet appartement, si le loyer (ÊTRE)
　moins élevé.
5　Nous prendrons cet appartement, si le propriétaire
　(ACCEPTER) de baisser le loyer.
6　Si nous (HABITER) ici, je pourrais prendre le métro tous les jours.

B›› Complete the sentences below by putting the verb in brackets into the correct tense.

1   Si nous ne pouvons pas trouver un appartement en plein centre, nous (ESSAYER) d'acheter une maison en banlieue.
2   J'aimerais beaucoup habiter dans ce quartier si les loyers (ÊTRE) moins élevés.
3   Je serais prêt à louer l'appartement au cinquième étage si l'immeuble (AVOIR) un ascenseur.
4   Si nous (LOUER) cet appartement, nous pourrons économiser un peu d'argent.

○   si meaning *whether* can be followed by any tense:

Je ne sais pas **si** nous avons les moyens d'acheter un tel appartement.
I don't know if we can afford to buy a flat like that.

Je ne sais pas **si** je voudrais vivre ici.
I don't know if I would want to live here.

Je ne sais pas **si** j'aurais choisi de vivre en banlieue.
I don't know if I would have chosen to live in the suburbs.

○   Note that **si** shortens to **s'** only when followed by **il** and **ils**:
s'il veut vivre... **s'ils** veulent vivre...
but:
si elle veut vivre... si elles veulent vivre...

○   Note also that **si on** sometimes changes to **si l'on**.

7.6 *Ce, cet, cette, ces*

ce quartier
cette maison
ces immeubles
cet appartement

○   To translate *this/that* use **ce, cet, cette**, and for *these/those* use **ces**. Look carefully at these examples:

– Tu aimes le quartier où nous habitons?
Do you like the area we live in?

– Oui, j'adore **ce** quartier.
Yes, I love this area.

– Comment trouves-tu la pièce?
What do you think of the room?
– J'aime beaucoup **cette pièce**.
I like this room a lot.

– Alors, tu préfères les appartements modernes?
Do you prefer modern flats?
– Ah oui, **ces appartements** sont très spacieux.
Yes, these flats are very spacious.

The rule is therefore:

le	→	ce
la	→	cette
les	→	ces

O The form **cet** is used only with masculine words which begin with a vowel or a mute h, in order to avoid the sound gap that would be caused by ce.

ce + appartement → **cet** appartement
ce + immeuble → **cet** immeuble

〉〉 Fill in the correct form of **ce, cet, cette,** or **ces**.

1 ___ chambre serait idéale pour les enfants.
2 ___ immeubles sont très prestigieux.
3 ___ vieille cheminée est très belle.
4 ___ pièces sont beaucoup trop petites.
5 ___ supermarché vend tous les produits essentiels.
6 ___ maison à Versailles était beaucoup trop chère.
7 ___ agence est ouverte jusqu'à neuf heures.
8 Je n'aime pas ___ rideaux.
9 Quels appartements allons-nous visiter ___ après-midi?
10 ___ évier est en très mauvais état.
11 Il vaudrait mieux jeter ___ vieux tapis.
12 ___ agent connaît bien le quartier.

7.7 *Celui, celle, ceux, celles*

> **Celui de la rue de Fontenay**
>
> **Celui qui donnait sur le bois de Vincennes.**
> **Celui que nous avons visité hier.**
>
> **Celui-ci est un peu plus grand.**
> **Celui-là est au troisième.**

○ To translate *the one who/which, the ones who/which* use **celui qui/que, celle qui/que, ceux qui/que,** or **celles qui/que**, depending on whether what is being referred to is masculine, feminine, singular or plural.

Look at these examples:

– Quel appartement? (masculine singular) *Which flat?*
– **Celui qui** est au troisième étage.
The one that's on the third floor.

– Quelle pièce? (feminine singular) *Which room?*
– **Celle qui** est à côté de la cuisine.
The one that's next to the kitchen.

– Quels locataires? (masculine plural) *Which tenants?*
– **Ceux qui** sont au-dessous de nous.
The ones that live down below.

– Quelles fenêtres? (feminine plural) *Which windows?*
– **Celles qui** donnent sur la rue.
The ones that look out over the street.

A》 Complete the answers to the following questions by using **celui, celle, ceux** or **celles**.

1   Quelle fenêtre? – ___ qui donne sur la cour.
2   Quels rideaux? – ___ qui sont dans la salle de séjour.
3   Quel tapis? – ___ qui est dans l'entrée.
4   Quel appartement? – ___ que nous avons vu hier.
5   Quelles lampes? – ___ que nous avons vues au BHV samedi.
6   Quels tableaux? – ___ que tes parents nous ont donnés.

○ **Celui, celle, ceux, celles** can also be used with **-ci** and **-là** to mean *this one* and *that one, these* and *those*:

> Quel tissu préfères-tu? **Celui-ci** ou **celui-là**?
>
> *Which material do you prefer? This one or that one?*
>
> Quelle lampe préfères-tu? **Celle-ci** ou **celle-là**?
>
> *Which lamp do you like best? This one or that one?*
>
> Quels éléments préfères-tu? **Ceux-ci** ou **ceux-là**?
>
> *Which units do you prefer? These or those?*
>
> Quelles chaises préfères-tu? **Celles-ci** ou **celles-là**?
>
> *Which chairs do you like best? These or those?*

○ **Celui, celle, ceux, celles** can be used with **de** to mean *the one/the ones belonging to*.

> Quel appartement? – **Celui de** tes parents.
> Quelle cuisine? – **Celle de** tante Marianne.
> Quels rideaux? – **Ceux de** la salle de bains.
> Quelles chaises? – **Celles de** la salle à manger.

○ There is sometimes confusion between **cela (ça)** which conveys the idea of *this, that,* or *it* as a general idea and **celui, celle, ceux** and **celles** which all refer back to a particular noun that has been previously used. Remember that **celui, celle, ceux, celles** are always followed by one of the following patterns:

i. **-ci** or **-là**
ii. **de, du, de la, de l'**, or **des**
iii. **qui** or **que**

B》 Use **cela** or **celui, celle, ceux, celles**, as appropriate in the following sentences.

1 Quel appartement préfères-tu? – ___ de la rue Monge.
2 Je n'aimerais pas vivre là. ___ ne me plairait pas du tout.
3 Quelle pièce va servir de séjour? – ___ qui donne sur la place.
4 Tu veux chercher un appartement en banlieue? – Non, ___ ne m'intéresse pas.

5 Tu préférerais habiter un appartement près du centre? – Oui,
___ me permettrait de partir plus tard le matin.

6 Quel appartement est le moins cher? – ___ que nous avons
visité mardi soir.

7.8 How to translate *which...?* and *which one?*

> Quel appartement préférez-vous?
> Lequel préférez-vous?

○ **Quel...?** *(which...?)* is an adjective and is therefore always used
with a noun. It has four forms, according to whether the noun is
masculine (m) or feminine (f), singular (s) or plural (pl):

Quel appartement?	(m.s.)	*Which flat?*
Quelle pièce?	(f.s.)	*Which room?*
Quels éléments?	(m.pl.)	*Which units?*
Quelles chaises?	(f.pl.)	*Which chairs?*

○ **Lequel?** *(which one?)* is a pronoun and is therefore used **without a
noun**. Its four forms are:

Lequel?	(m.s.)	*Which one?*
Laquelle?	(f.s.)	*Which one?*
Lesquels?	(m.pl.)	*Which ones?*
Lesquelles?	(f.pl)	*Which ones?*

– J'ai visité l'appartement.	*I visited the flat.*
– L'appartement? **Lequel**?	*The flat? Which one?*
– Celui de la rue de Verdun.	*The one in the rue de Verdun.*
– J'aime bien ces chaises.	*I quite like those chairs.*
– **Lesquelles**?	*Which ones?*
– Celles qui sont dans le grenier.	*The ones which are in the attic.*

» Use the correct form of **quel** or **lequel** to complete the following sentences.

1   ___ plantes vas-tu acheter pour la cuisine?
2   ___ des deux appartements préfères-tu?
3   ___ des pièces te semble préférable?
4   ___ pièce choisirais-tu pour la chambre des enfants?
5   ___ tableaux veux-tu mettre dans le salon?
6   Voici deux tissus. ___ préfères-tu?

8 Making longer statements

On aurait mieux mangé si on était resté à la maison.

The Mermet family discuss the inadequate nouvelle cuisine meal they've just had at an expensive restaurant.

M. Mermet:	Quel désastre que ce repas! Ce n'était pas du tout ce que **j'avais prévu**.	8.1
Mme Mermet:	**On aurait mieux mangé** si **on était resté** à la maison.	8.2 / 8.4 / 8.1

Michel:	**On aurait certainement mieux mangé si on était allé** dans un restaurant fast-food!	8.2 / 8.4 / 8.1
M. Mermet:	N'exagérons pas, Michel! **J'avais voulu vous offrir à tous quelque chose de différent, quelque chose d'exceptionnel**.	8.1 8.8 / 8.11 8.11
Michel:	Et c'était vraiment **quelque chose de différent**.Je n'ai jamais vu **des portions si petites**! Alors que **si on avait mangé** un hamburger...! Il n'y **a rien de plus appétissant**!	8.11 8.9 8.1 8.11
M. Mermet:	J'en ai assez de tes hamburgers! Mais une chose est certaine: **si on était allé** dans un restaurant fast-food, **le repas aurait coûté** beaucoup moins cher!	8.1 8.2
Mme Mermet:	Et le service laissait beaucoup à désirer. **Le garçon était si maladroit** et **de si mauvaise humeur**. J'avais même l'impression **qu'il avait un peu trop bu**.	8.9 / 8.3 8.1 8.12
M. Mermet:	Quand il m'a présenté l'addition, j'ai cru qu'il **s'était trompé. Cela m'étonne qu'on soit prêt** à pratiquer **de tels prix**.	8.12 / 8.1 8.5 / 8.7 8.9
Michel:	Bon, Résumons! **Personne n'a mangé** à sa faim. **Rien n'était satisfaisant. Ni la cuisine ni le service n'étaient bons. Pour bien manger il vaudrait mieux** aller chez McDonald.	8.10 8.10 8.3 8.4
Mme Mermet:	Ou bien **rester chez soi** et **faire la cuisine soi-même**.	8.5
M. Mermet:	Pour moi, **la bonne cuisine traditionnelle est meilleure** que cette nouvelle cuisine. En France, **on mange de plus en plus mal**. Si **on avait servi un repas si léger** et présenté **une addition si élevée** il y a 20 ans, **on aurait refusé** de la payer. Moi, **je n'ai pas l'habitude de me plaindre**, mais cette fois, **je vais envoyer une lettre à la Chambre de Commerce**.	8.3 8.4 8.5 / 8.3 8.1 / 8.9 8.9 / 8.5 8.6 8.8
Michel:	Et la prochaine fois, **on ira** dîner dans un restaurant fast-food!	8.5

8.1 The pluperfect tense

> **il avait bu**
> **on était allé**
> **il s'était trompé**

○ The pluperfect tense is used to convey the idea of what someone *had done*. For example:

> M. Mermet était fâché parce qu'il **avait espéré** offrir à sa famille un repas exceptionnel.
> *M. Mermet was annoyed because he had hoped to give his family a special treat.*

○ The pluperfect is formed by putting together the ***imperfect of the auxiliary verb*** (i.e. the imperfect of avoir or être) **+ *the past participle***. Look at the three basic forms below:

> M. Mermet **avait payé** très cher un repas médiocre.
> *M. Mermet had paid a lot for a very ordinary meal.*

> Michel **était allé** dans un fast-food à midi.
> *Michel had been to a fast-food restaurant at lunch-time.*

> Le garçon **s'était trompé** en faisant l'addition.
> *The waiter had made a mistake with the bill.*

○ Note that the rule for perfect tense agreements applies here too:

> Mme Mermet était rest**ée** à la maison toute la journée.
> Les Mermet s'étaient installé**s** près de la porte.

○ Once you have mastered the three basic forms above, you should be able to fit in the variations fairly easily:

> Si seulement j'avais consulté mes collègues...
> Si seulement tu avais lu le guide Gault et Millau...
> Si seulement nous avions choisi un restaurant traditionnel...
> Si seulement vous n'aviez pas mangé à midi...
> Si seulement les desserts avaient été meilleurs...

A⟩⟩ Using the verbs given below, complete the sentences with a suitable verb in the pluperfect tense. Try to translate the sentences as you go.

servir	devoir	recommander	manger	passer
aller	coûter	espérer	faire	être

Les Mermet étaient déçus de leur soirée au restaurant...

...parce qu'on leur ___ ___ (**1**) un repas très léger.

...parce que le repas ___ ___ (**2**) très ordinaire et il ___ ___ (**3**) cher aussi.

...parce qu'ils ___ ___ (**4**) s'installer près de la porte.

...parce que M. Mermet ___ ___ (**5**) offrir à sa famille un repas exceptionnel.

...parce que le garçon ___ très mal ___ (**6**) son travail.

...parce qu'ils n' ___ pas ___ (**7**) à leur faim.

...parce qu'ils ___ ___ (**8**) au restaurant pour manger quelque chose d'exceptionnel.

...parce qu'un collègue de M. Mermet ___ ___ (**9**) la cuisine et le service.

...parce qu'ils ___ ___ (**10**) une soirée peu agréable.

B⟩⟩ Complete these sentences, using the pluperfect tense of a suitable verb chosen from the box below.

aller	inventer	faire	dîner	prendre	manger
préparer	choisir	être	servir		

1 ...si on ___ ___ dans un restaurant fast-food.

2 ...si on ___ ___ un hamburger-frites.

3 ...si M. Mermet ___ ___ le repas lui-même.

4 ...si le Globe d'Or ___ ___ des repas plus copieux.

5 ...si on ___ ___ plus attention à la quantité qu'à la présentation.

6 ...si on ___ ___ un bon restaurant traditionnel.

7 ...si le garçon ___ ___ plus attentif.

8 ...si on ___ ___ dans une pizzeria.

9 ...si on ___ ___ à la maison.

10 ...si Paul Bocuse n'___ pas ___ la nouvelle cuisine!

Si seulement tu n'avais pas mangé à midi...

8.2 The conditional perfect tense

> on aurait mangé
> on serait allé
> on se serait amusé

○ The conditional perfect tense is made up of the conditional of the auxiliary verb (avoir or être) plus the past participle.

avoir verbs:	j'aurais mangé
être verbs:	je serais allé
reflexive verbs:	je me serais amusé

>> The Mermet family explain what they would have done instead of going to the smart restaurant.
Put the verbs in brackets into the conditional perfect tense.

1 M. Mermet (CHOISIR) un petit restaurant traditionnel. Cela (COÛTER) moins cher et on (MANGER) mieux.
2 Mme. Mermet (PRÉPARER) un repas spécial à la maison. Elle (ACHETER) de bonnes petites choses chez Fauchon.
3 "Nous (MIEUX FAIRE) de rester à la maison," a-t-elle dit.
4 "Je (PRÉFÉRER) manger dans un fast-food," a affirmé Michel. "Je (ALLER) au McDo au centre-ville," a-t-il ajouté.
5 Lui et son ami (SORTIR) en ville. Ils (S'AMUSER) bien.

8.3 How to translate *good*, *bad*, *well* and *badly*

> – Le service était bon?
> – Non, il était très mauvais.
> – Vous avez bien mangé?
> – Non, on mange de plus en plus mal en France.

○ Remember that the words for *good* and *bad* are adjectives and must therefore agree with the noun they describe: use **bon, bonne, bons, bonnes** (*good*), or **mauvais, mauvaise, mauvais, mauvaises** (*bad*).

○ *Well* and *badly* are adverbs and therefore do not change: use **bien** *(well)* or **mal** *(badly)*.

›› Complete this passage about eating in France by filling in the gaps with the appropriate French word for *good, bad, well* or *badly*.

J'aime beaucoup manger en France. La cuisine française est très _____ (**1**). En général, on mange très _____ (**2**) et le service est _____ (**3**) aussi. Il est rare de manger un _____ (**4**) repas.

Malheureusement, au Globe d'Or le service était _____ (**5**). Le garçon était de _____ (**6**) humeur et il faisait _____ (**7**) son travail. Il mettait tout au _____ (**8**) endroit, il versait _____ (**9**) le vin et il parlait si _____ (**10**) que les Mermet ne comprenaient pas _____ (**11**) ce qu'il disait.

Selon M. Mermet, la cuisine traditionnelle est très _____ (**12**) mais il pense au contraire que les hamburgers sont très _____ (**13**) pour la santé. Il pense aussi qu'on mange _____ (**14**) à la maison. Il aime _____ (**15**) les _____ (**16**) petits repas qu'il fait le week-end.

8.4 How to translate *better*

> La cuisine traditionnelle est meilleure.
> On aurait mieux mangé à la maison.

○ There are two words in French for *better*: **meilleur** and **mieux**.

Meilleur is an adjective and must agree with the noun it describes:

> Le service est **meilleur** chez Lucien.
> *The service is better at Lucien's.*

> La cuisine traditionnelle est **meilleure**.
> *Traditional food is better.*

Mieux is an adverb and does not change:

> On mange **mieux** en France que n'importe quel autre pays européen.
> *You eat better in France than in any other European country.*

》 Some advice on how to find the best restaurants in France –
provided you have the necessary funds! Complete this text using
meilleur, meilleure, meilleurs, meilleures or **mieux** as
appropriate.

Quelques-uns des _____ (**1**) restaurants français sont en province
mais pour être sûr d'en trouver un, il vaudrait _____ (**2**) aller à Paris
où chaque chef de cuisine s'efforce de créer les _____ (**3**) plats et
de les présenter _____ (**4**) que tous les autres chefs.
Les _____ (**5**) restaurants sont souvent visités par les inspecteurs
du guide Michelin qui accordent des étoiles, trois pour les _____
(**6**) restaurants de France. C'est là qu'on mange le _____ (**7**), c'est
là qu'on boit les _____ (**8**) vins, on vous sert _____ (**9**) qu'ailleurs,
mais c'est là aussi qu'il vaudrait _____ (**10**) avoir un portefeuille
bien garni. Dans le Michelin on trouve aussi les _____ (**11**) plats
que chacun des _____ (**12**) établissements offre à ses clients. M.
Mermet ne fréquente pas ces établissements: il aime _____ (**13**) les
petits restaurants où on sert la cuisine traditionnelle qui est, selon
lui, bien _____ (**14**) que la nouvelle cuisine.

8.5 How to use *on*

> On peut faire la cuisine soi-même.

○ **On** is basically similar to *one* in English, but is much more widely
used in French and can also be translated as *we, you, people in general.*
Look at these examples using **on**, and note how **son**, **sa**, **ses**, **soi**,
and **vous** are used with it.

> **On** peut facilement préparer son dîner en une demi-heure.
> **On** peut manger à sa faim. **On** peut choisir ses aliments avec
> soin.
> *You can easily get your evening meal in half an hour. You can eat as
> much as you like. You can choose your food carefully.*

> Il est facile de préparer ses repas **soi-même**.
> *It's easy to prepare meals oneself.*

> Souvent, on préfère rester **chez soi** manger dans une
> ambiance décontractée.
> *One often prefers to stay at home and eat in a relaxed atmosphere.*

Si un ami vous invite à dîner au restaurant, on doit offrir de payer sa part.
If a friend invites one to have a meal in a restaurant, one has to offer to pay one's share.

>> Complete this text about meals at home and eating out. Fill the gaps with **son, sa, ses, soi,** or **vous,** as appropriate. The examples above will help you.

Pour le petit déjeuner, on peut préparer _____ (1) café et _____ (2) tartines _____ (3) -même.
À midi, on peut aller dans _____ (4) café préféré. Souvent, un collège ou un ami _____ (5) invite à prendre un verre avec lui. Le soir, généralement, on préfère manger chez _____ (6).
Naturellement, de temps en temps, pour fêter _____ (7) anniversaire ou celui de _____ (8) femme ou de _____ (9) enfants, on est content de sortir de chez _____ (10) pour manger un bon petit repas dans le restaurant de _____ (11) choix. C'est bien d'avoir _____ (12) famille autour de _____ (13) même si _____ (14) portefeuille s'en trouve considérablement allégé!

8.6 Reflexive verbs (in the infinitive form)

je n'ai pas l'habitude de me plaindre

O   When using reflexive verbs in the infinitive form, remember to use the correct reflexive pronoun. Look at these examples:

– Tu veux **t'asseoir** à la terrasse?
– *Do you want to sit outside?*

– Je préfère **m'installer** à l'intérieur.
– *I prefer to sit inside.*
– Vous voulez **vous asseoir** là-bas?
– *Would you like to sit over there?*

– Nous allons **nous offrir** un bon petit repas.
– *We're going to treat ourselves to a nice meal.*

>> Complete the following sentences by adding the appropriate reflexive pronoun.

Nous avons voulu _____ (**1**) installer dans un petit coin agréable mais la table était réservée et nous avons dû _____ (**2**) asseoir près de la porte.
Voulez-vous _____ (**3**) mettre à table, messieurs-dames?
Voulez-vous _____ (**4**) asseoir ici, monsieur?
Michel, tu veux _____ (**5**) asseoir à côté de moi?
Je ne peux pas _____ (**6**) habituer à cette nouvelle cuisine.
On trouve difficile de _____ (**7**) adapter à ces nouvelles habitudes alimentaires.
Tu vas _____ (**8**) plaindre auprès du patron?

8.7 Expressions of emotion + subjunctive

> Cela m'étonne qu'on soit prêt à pratiquer de tels prix.

O Nearly all verbs and phrases expressing emotion, except espérer (*to hope*), are followed by a verb in the subjunctive. Here are a few examples:

Il est dommage que la cuisine traditionnelle **soit** moins à la mode aujourd'hui.
It's a pity that traditional food is less popular nowadays.

Cela m'étonne qu'un restaurateur **ait** le culot de pratiquer des prix si élevés.
I'm surprised that a restaurant has the cheek to charge such high prices.

Je suis content que vous **puissiez** venir dîner chez nous samedi.
I'm pleased that you can come to dinner on Saturday.

>> Complete these sentences with the correct form of the verb in brackets.

1   Cela m'étonne qu'on (FAIRE) un tel effort pour préparer un repas si ordinaire.
2   Il est dommage que la cuisine traditionnelle ne (ÊTRE) plus à la mode.

3 Cela m'étonne que tant de gens (ALLER) dans les restaurants de fast-food.

4 Il est dommage que tout le monde (CHOISIR) toujours les mêmes plats.

5 Cela m'étonne que les gens (SORTIR) si souvent au restaurant puisque cela coûte si cher.

6 Il est dommage que les jeunes ne (SAVOIR) pas apprécier la qualité de la cuisine traditionnelle.

7 Cela m'étonne que les Français (PRENDRE) la cuisine tellement au sérieux.

8 Je suis content que toute la famille (AVOIR) son mot à dire sur le repas.

8.8 To give someone something = *donner quelque chose à quelqu'un*

j'avais voulu vous offrir à tous un bon repas
je vais envoyer une lettre à la Chambre de Commerce

○ With verbs like *give* (donner), *show* (montrer), *offer* (offrir), *send* (envoyer), the idea of *to* is often omitted in English. In French the à has to be included each time. Look at these examples:

Il a donné un pourboire **au garçon**.
He gave the waiter a tip.

Il a montré l'addition **à sa femme**.
He showed his wife the bill.

Les restaurants traditionnels offrent **à leurs clients** de bons repas.
Traditional restaurants offer their customers good meals.

≫ Translate these sentences into French.

1 The waiter gave the Mermets the menu and the wine list.
2 The waiter gave Michel a small portion of chips.
3 He offered M. Mermet another glass of wine.
4 M. Mermet showed the bill to the waiter.

5   He didn't give the waiter a tip.
6   Many restaurants offer the customer a good choice of food.
7   Mme Mermet gave her son some money to buy a hamburger.
8   M. Mermet sent the Chamber of Commerce a letter.

8.9 How to translate *such*

Je n'ai jamais mangé un tel repas.
Je n'ai jamais payé si cher un repas si léger.

○   There are two ways of saying *such* in French: by using **tel** or **si**. Look at these examples:

Je n'ai jamais mangé un **tel** repas!
I've never eaten such a meal!

Je n'ai jamais mangé un repas **si** copieux!
I've never eaten such a big meal!

Tel is used with a noun and has to agree. The forms are: **tel**, **telle**, **tels**, and **telles**.

Si is used if the phrase already includes an adjective with a noun.

A》 Complete these sentences using **tel**, **telle**, **tels** or **telles**.

1   Quel repas! Je n'ai jamais mangé un ___
2   Quelle addition! Je n'ai jamais payé une ___
3   Quelle sauce! Je n'ai jamais goûté une ___

B》 Complete these sentences using **si**.

1   Quel garçon maladroit! Je n'ai jamais rencontré un ___
2   Quelle soirée désagréable! Je n'ai jamais passé une ___
3   Quelle petite portion! On ne m'a jamais servi une ___

8.10 *Personne ne..., rien ne...*

Personne n'a bien mangé.
Rien n'était satisfaisant.

○ You are probably familiar with the use of the negative in sentences like 'Je n'ai rencontré personne' and 'Je n'ai rien mangé'.

○ Note that personne and rien can also be used as the subject of a verb:

Personne n'a mangé à sa faim.
Nobody had enough to eat.

Rien n'était satisfaisant.
Nothing was satisfactory.

≫ M. Mermet has very fixed ideas on good, wholesome home cooking. Rephrase his comments, starting each sentences with **rien** or **personne**.

1 Il n'y a rien de moins sain qu'un hamburger. Rien n' ___
2 Il n'y a personne de si désagréable qu'un serveur maladroit. Personne ___
3 Il n'y a personne qui cuisine mieux que ma femme.
4 Il n'y a rien de plus satisfaisant qu'un plat traditionnel.
5 Il n'y a rien qui attire les jeunes autant qu'un Big Mac.
6 Il n'y a personne qui mange plus mal qu'un adolescent américain.

8.11 *Quelque chose, quelqu'un, rien, personne + de*

quelque chose de différent
quelque chose d'exceptionnel
il n'y a rien de plus appétissant

○ The masculine singular form of the adjective is used after the **de**.

Quelque chose de différent. *Something different.*
Quelqu'un de sympathique. *Someone nice.*
Rien de spécial. *Nothing special.*
Personne d'autre. *Nobody else.*

>> Rephrase the following sentences.

1 J'aime manger des plats exotiques.
   J'aime manger quelque chose ___

2 Quelquefois on veut impressionner un client important.
   Quelquefois on veut impressionner quelqu'un ___

3 Je préfère des plats simples et savoureux.
   Je préfère quelque chose ___

○ Note the word order when words such as **si**, **plus** and **moins** are added:

> Quelque chose de plus/moins cher.
> *Something more/less expensive.*
> Rien de si intéressant.
> *Nothing so interesting.*

>> Rephrase the following sentences

1 Rien n'est plus agréable qu'un dîner entre amis.
   Il n'y a rien ___

2 Personne n'est si désagréable qu'un serveur inattentif et maladroit.
   Il n'y a personne ___

3 Rien n'est moins appétissant qu'un hamburger graisseux!
   Il n'y a rien ___

8.12 Direct and indirect speech

> "Il a trop bu."
> **J'avais l'impression qu'il avait trop bu.**

○ "Je préfère le fast-food" is direct speech (Michel's actual words). Michel a dit qu'il préférait le fast-food, is indirect speech (reporting what Michel said).

Here are two more examples.

>
> Direct speech: "J'ai mangé un meilleur repas à la cantine à midi."
>
> Indirect speech: Michel a dit qu'il avait mangé un meilleur repas à midi.

>> Turn the sentences below into indirect speech, using the imperfect or pluperfect tense as appropriate.

1 "Il y a une erreur dans l'addition" a dit M. Mermet.
2 "Ce n'est pas possible" a répliqué le serveur.
3 "Nous avons pris une bouteille de vin, pas deux" a ajouté M. Mermet.
4 "C'est vrai" a avoué le serveur.
5 "Je vais corriger l'addition" a-t-il ajouté.
6 "Il a trop bu" a noté Mme Mermet.
7 "Il a oublié d'apporter les verres" a-t-elle expliqué.

○ Note how the speaking verb in these sentences is inverted after speech:

...a dit M. Mermet and **a-t-il ajouté**

>> Rephrase the following sentences, using direct speech and putting the speaking verb at the end of the sentence.

1 M. Mermet a dit qu'un de ses collègues avait recommandé le restaurant.
2 Il a ajouté qu'il s'était vraiment trompé.
3 Mme Mermet a expliqué que le garçon avait fait plusieurs erreurs.
4 Elle a dit qu'il avait trop bu.
5 J'ai dit que j'avais déjà mangé à midi.
6 J'ai ajouté que j'avais déjeuné dans la cantine du collège.
7 Michel a demandé pourquoi son père avait choisi ce restaurant.
8 Il a dit que lui, il préférait le fast-food.

9 Being at the receiving end of and expressing negative reactions

M. Bernard talks about his son's poor mental and physical condition after a very serious car accident.

M. Roy:	Votre fils? Il va mieux aujourd'hui?	
M. Bernard:	Pas vraiment. **J'ai peur qu'il ne soit très malade**. Il a très mauvaise mine. Quand je l'ai vu hier soir, **j'ai été bouleversé. J'ai été effrayé** par sa pâleur. **Il n'a rien mangé** depuis trois jours. **Il ne veut rien boire** non plus. **Il ne veut voir personne** sauf sa femme. Et **elle ne peut pas aller** le voir. **L'odeur des hôpitaux la rend malade**. Tout va très mal.	9.5 9.1 9.2 9.2 9.2 9.2 / 9.6 9.4
M. Roy:	On vous a expliqué comment l'accident s'est produit?	

Je n'ai aucune envie de conduire.

M. Bernard:	**Je n'en sais rien**. Il rentrait de Dunkerque assez tard le soir avec deux de ses collègues. Il y avait du brouillard sur l'autoroute du Nord et la voiture est entrée en collision avec un camion... **Ils auraient dû passer** la nuit à Dunkerque mais **Pierre n'a jamais aimé changer** de programme. **Les autres passagers ont été tués** sur le coup et **la voiture a été gravement endommagée**. **Cela m'étonne que Pierre en ait réchappé**. **Il a été transporté** d'urgence à l'hôpital de Péronne et **il a dû être opéré** tout de suite. **Si son état ne s'améliore pas, il va être transféré** à l'hôpital Cochin à Paris.	9.2 9.6 9.2 / 9.6 9.1 9.1 9.5 9.1 9.6 / 9.1 9.2 9.1 / 9.6
M. Roy:	**Peut-être qu'il va mieux** que vous ne pensez. J'espère que votre fils ira mieux quand **vous irez le voir** ce soir.	9.3 9.6
M. Bernard:	Moi, je fais ce que je peux, mais **j'ai peur que Pierre ne se remette jamais** de cet accident. Il a encore de gros problèmes à surmonter.	9.5 9.2

9.1 The passive

> **J'ai été bouleversé.**
> **Il a été transporté à l'hôpital.**
> **Les autres passagers ont été tués.**

○ The passive in French follows the same pattern as the passive in English. Compare the examples below:

> En France, le traitement médical **est payé** par l'individu.
> *In France medical treatment is paid for by the individual.*

> Plus tard, le coût **sera remboursé** par la Sécurité social.
> *Later the cost will be refunded by the State.*

> Pierre **a été blessé** dans un accident de la route.
> *Pierre has been injured in a car accident.*

> On a dit à M. Bernard que Pierre **serait opéré** tout de suite.
> *They told M. Bernard that Pierre would be operated on right away.*

> On lui a dit que Pierre **avait été transféré** à l'hôpital Cochin.
> *They told him that Pierre had been transferred to the Hôpital Cochin.*

○ You can see that the passive in French is made up of the verb **être** in the relevant tense + *__the past participle__* just as the English passive is made up of the verb *to be* + **the *past participle.***

○ This rule also applies when an infinitive is used:

> **Il va être opéré** tout de suite.
> *He is going to be operated on right away.*

> **Il doit être transféré** dans un hôpital parisien.
> *He's got to be transferred to a Paris hospital.*

○ Note that since the passive always involves the use of **être**, the past participle always has to agree with the subject of the sentence:

> La sécurité routière est **assurée** par la Gendarmerie Nationale.
> *Road safety is supervised by the Gendarmerie Nationale.*

> Les autoroutes sont **gérées** par une société privée.
> *The motorways are run by a private company.*

○ Watch out especially when you have to express ideas like: *'His son was killed in a car accident'*. Since the son was only killed once, the perfect passive must be used: **Son fils a été tué** dans un accident de la route. (**Son fils était tué** would mean that his son was killed more than once, every morning, for example!) Similarly: *'The other passengers were seriously injured'*: = **Les autres passagers ont été gravement blessés**.

A⟩⟩ Rephrase this text replacing the underlined sections with the perfect passive. For example:

On a construit beaucoup d'autoroutes.
Beaucoup d'autoroutes **ont été construites**.

Dans les années 60 et 70, on a pris (**1**) toutes sortes de mesures pour réglementer la circulation automobile à Paris. On a mis (**2**) certaines rues en sens unique. On a créé (**3**) des zones à stationnement limité. On a installé (**4**) des parcmètres et on a embauché (**5**) des contractuels pour faire observer les règlements. L'automobiliste parisien a accepté (**6**) ces mesures à contre-coeur. En même temps, on a fait (**7**) des efforts pour rendre sa vie plus facile. On a aménagé (**8**) de nombreux parkings souterrains et on a entrepris (**9**) de grands travaux routiers. On a créé (**10**) une voie express le long de la rive droite de la Seine et, en 1970, on a mis (**11**) en service le Boulevard Périphérique. De plus, on a construit (**12**) de nombreuses autoroutes pour améliorer les liaisons routières avec le reste de la France.

B⟩⟩ Now translate the whole text into English.

○ A certain number of verbs cannot be used in the passive in quite the same way as in English. They are all verbs that are followed by **à**, for example, **donner, offrir, demander, dire, permettre**. Instead of using the passive with such verbs, we have to use **on + the active form of the verb**. Look at these examples:

> **On lui a donné** une auto pour son anniversaire.
> *He was given a car for his birthday./They gave him a car for his birthday.*

> **On ne permettait pas** à Caroline de sortir en semaine.
> *Caroline was not allowed to go out during the week./They didn't allow Caroline to go out during the week.*

> **On m'a dit** de revenir le lendemain.
> *I was told to come back the next day./They told me to come back the next day.*

C)» Translate the following sentences into French, using the verbs given below. (They all take **à + the person involved**.)

offrir	donner	demander	permettre	conseiller

1 When Pierre was offered his new job, he was given a faster car. (perfect tense)
2 He was allowed to use it at the weekend too. (imperfect tense)
3 He was often asked to take colleagues to Paris. (imperfect tense)
4 That particular day, he was advised to leave early because there was fog on the motorway. (perfect tense)

9.2 The negative

Il n'a jamais aimé les voitures.
Il ne veut rien boire.
Il ne veut voir personne.

○ Look at the negative phrases in these sentences about the long-term effects of Pierre's accident:

Depuis son accident, **Pierre ne va nulle part** en voiture.
Since his accident Pierre goes nowhere by car.

Il n'a aucune envie de conduire.
He has no desire to drive.

En fait, **il n'a plus** de voiture.
In fact, he no longer has a car.

Il ne dit rien quand on parle de voitures.
He says nothing when people talk about cars.

Il ne parle jamais de son accident.
He never talks about his accident.

Il croit que **son cas n'intéresse personne**.
He thinks that his situation doesn't interest anybody.

Note how the negatives are placed around the verb: **ne** before the verb and the other part of the negative phrase after the verb.

○ In the perfect tense, most negatives go either side of the auxiliary verb:

Il n'a pas expliqué ce qui est arrivé ce soir-là.
He hasn't explained what happened that evening.

Il n'a rien dit sur les causes de l'accident.
He has said nothing about the causes of the accident.

Il n'a jamais parlé de ses collègues.
He has never spoken about his colleagues.

Il n'a plus voulu acheter de voiture.
He hasn't wanted to buy another car.

○ With some negative phrases in the perfect tense, however, the second part of the negative phrase comes after the past participle:

ne...personne *(nobody)*, **ne...nulle part** *(nowhere)*, **ne...aucun(e)** *(not any)* and **ne...que** *(only)*:

Il n'a critiqué personne.
He hasn't criticised anyone.

Depuis son accident, **il n'est allé nulle part** en voiture.
Since his accident he hasn't travelled anywhere by car.

Il n'a manifesté aucune envie d'avoir une voiture.
He has shown no desire to have a car.

》 Answer these questions about Pierre with a whole sentence which includes the negative words supplied in brackets.

1 Sa femme est venue à l'hôpital? (ne...jamais)
2 Il a acheté une autre voiture? (ne...plus)
3 Il a accusé les autres conducteurs d'avoir causé l'accident? (ne...personne)
4 Il a essayé d'expliquer l'accident? (ne...jamais)
5 Il a fait quelque chose pour aider les enfants de ses collègues? (ne...rien)
6 Il a critiqué les médecins? (ne...personne)
7 Il a fait des exercices pour se remettre en forme? (ne...rien)
8 Il est allé en vacances pour se changer les idées? (ne...nulle part)

○ When using negatives with infinitives, the same pattern applies as with the auxiliary verb in the perfect tense. Look at these examples. Translate them into English. Then translate them back into French:

Il ne veut pas manger.
Il ne veut rien manger.
Il ne veut plus conduire de voiture.
Il ne veut jamais sortir le week-end.

BUT:

Il ne veut voir personne.
Il ne veut voir aucun membre de la famille de ses collègues.
Il ne veut aller nulle part en voiture.

9.3 How to use *peut-être*

peut-être qu'il va mieux

○ There are three different ways of using the word **peut-être** *(perhaps)*. Look at these examples showing how *'Perhaps Pierre will be better this evening'* can be translated:

If **peut-être** is used at the beginning of the sentence, the verb and subject must be inverted:

Peut-être Pierre **ira-t-il** mieux ce soir.

If you use **peut-être que**, then no inversion is needed:

Peut-être que Pierre ira mieux ce soir.

Peut-être can be placed elsewhere in the sentence, but take care in complex sentences:

Pierre ira **peut-être** mieux ce soir.

≫ Write out the three versions of these sentences using **peut-être**.

1 La voiture a dérapé sur le verglas.
2 Pierre était un peu fatiqué.
3 Il y avait du brouillard sur l'autoroute.

9.4 *Rendre*

L'odeur des hôpital la rend malade.

○ Look at these examples showing how **rendre** can mean *to make*:

L'alcool **rend** les conducteurs irresponsables.
Alcohol makes drivers irresponsible.

Les bouchons sur le Périphérique **rendent** le trajet des banlieusards très fatigant.
The jams on the ring road make commuter travel very tiring.

>> Using the examples above as your model, translate the sentences below into French. Choose an appropriate adjective from the box below and don't forget to make the necessary agreements.

paresseux   facile   insupportable   sûr   dangereux   irrespirable

1   In winter fog makes motorways very dangerous.
    En hiver, le brouillard ___ les autoroutes très ___
2   Owning a car makes life easier.
    La possession d'une voiture ___ la vie plus ___
3   But cars make everybody very lazy.
    Mais les voitures ___ tout le monde très ___
4   Sometimes in towns the traffic makes the air difficult to breathe.
    Quelquefois en ville la circulation ___ l'air ___
5   Bad drivers make life unbearable for other people.
    Les mauvais conducteurs ___ la vie des autres ___
6   Speed limits make the roads safer.
    Les limitations de vitesse ___ les routes plus ___

9.5 Expressions of emotion + subjunctive

J'ai peur que Pierre ne soit très malade.

O   Look at these examples:

C'est dommage que sa femme ne **puisse** pas aller à l'hôpital.
It's a pity that his wife can't go to the hospital.

Je suis content qu'il **aille** mieux.
I'm glad he's better.

Cela m'étonne qu'il ne **veuille** pas voir ses amis.
I'm surprised that he doesn't want to see his friends.

J'ai peur qu'il ne **soit** très malade.
I'm afraid he's very ill.

These and all other expressions of emotion, **except** the verb **espérer** *(to hope)*, are followed by a clause with the verb in the subjunctive.

Note also that after **avoir peur que**... the verb in the subjunctive is preceded by **ne**.

>> Pierre's father is very concerned about his son. Complete what he says by putting the verbs in brackets into the correct form.

1   J'ai peur qu'il ne (ÊTRE) gravement blessé.

2   C'est dommage qu'il ne (VOULOIR) pas parler de son accident.

3   J'espère qu'il (ALLER) bientôt quitter l'hôpital.

4   C'est dommage qu'il ne (FAIRE) pas plus d'efforts pour marcher.

5   Je préfère qu'il ne (SAVOIR) pas pour le moment ce qui est arrivé à ses collègues.

6   J'ai peur qu'il ne (DEVENIR) fou en apprenant la vérité.

7   J'espère qu'il (POUVOIR) supporter ce choc.

8   J'ai peur qu'un visiteur ne lui (DIRE) exactement ce qui s'est passé.

9.6 Verbs + infinitive

Il ne veut rien boire.
J'hésite à lui parler de l'accident.
Il refuse de parler à la police.

○   Look at these examples:

> Elle **n'ose pas** le **voir**.
> *She doesn't dare to see him.*

> Il **a peur de conduire**.
> *He is afraid of driving.*

> Il **hésite à sortir**.
> *He hesitates to go out.*

See page 73 for general information on this point.

○   Look through the list below. Then cover it up and test yourself by writing out the correct version of the sentences that follow.

oser	– to dare to
sembler⎫	
paraître⎭	– to seem to

passer son temps à	– to spend time doing...
perdre son temps à	– to waste time doing...
hésiter à	– to hesitate to
renoncer à	– to give up doing...
avoir de la peine à ⎫	
avoir du mal à ⎬	– to have difficulty in doing...
avoir de la difficulté à ⎭	
se borner à	– to limit oneself to doing...
se contenter de	– to merely do...
cesser de	– to stop doing...
éviter de	– to avoid doing...
menacer de	– to threaten to
manquer de	– to fail to/to nearly do
refuser de	– to refuse to
risquer de	– to run the risk of doing...
oublier de	– to forget to
avoir peur de	– to be afraid to
empêcher quelqu'un de	– to prevent/stop someone doing...

>> Pierre's wife is really worried about him since his accident. Write out a correct version of what she says about him, by filling in the gaps with **de** or **à** where necessary.

1 Il n'ose pas ___ partir en vacances.
2 Il perd son temps ___ regarder la télévision toute la soirée.
3 Il se contente ___ changer de chaîne de temps en temps.
4 Il hésite ___ communiquer avec les autres.
5 Il a de la peine ___ parler avec ses collègues.
6 Il évite ___ leur parler autant que possible.
7 Il refuse ___ parler de l'accident.
8 Il semble ___ avoir peur ___ sortir.
9 Il a cessé ___ sortir le week-end.
10 Il se borne ___ regarder tout ce qu'il y a à la télévision.
11 Il a renoncé ___ conduire une voiture.
12 Il oublie quelquefois ___ se raser.
13 Il manque quelquefois ___ arriver au bureau à l'heure.
14 Il risque ___ perdre son emploi.
15 Il menace quelquefois ___ ne plus y aller.
16 Son état d'esprit l'empêche ___ mener une vie normale.

Now check your answers and learn the verbs you didn't get right.

10 An introduction to the subjunctive

Mes parents préfèrent que je sorte avec des gens qu'ils connaissent.

The dialogue below illustrates how the subjunctive is used. Read through the dialogue, analysing why the subjunctive is needed (see 10.1 and 10.4). To check the subjunctive forms, consult 10.2 and 10.3.

After some misunderstandings, Sylvie manages to persuade her father to let her go and spend a holiday with her friends in the South of France.

Sylvie: Ah, papa! **Mes amies veulent que je parte**[1] en vacances...

Père: Qu'est-ce que ça veut dire exactement, partir en vacances?

Sylvie: Une dizaine de mes amies...

Père: Non, Sylvie, **je ne crois pas que ce soit**[2] une bonne idée.

Sylvie: **Maman est d'accord que je parte**[3] comme ça. Mais **avant que je dise**[4] à mes amies que je peux y aller, **elle veut que tu sois**[5] aussi d'accord.

Père: Vraiment? **Elle accepte que des garçons et des filles partent**[6] comme ça? Moi, **je préfère que tu ailles**[7] en vacances avec nous **jusqu'à ce que tu aies**[8] **18 ans...**

Sylvie: Mais je crois que tu as mal compris. C'est un groupe de filles du lycée qui partent ensemble.

Père: Et je suppose que vous pensez faire du camping? Moi, **je n'aime pas que des filles fassent**[9] **du camping** toutes seules **sans qu'il y ait**[10] **quelqu'un qui puisse**[11] les surveiller un peu. **J'ai peur qu'un groupe de filles n'attire**[12] **les voyous** du pays. **Il faut que vous cherchiez**[13] **une autre solution qui puisse**[14] me satisfaire **avant que je te permette**[15] de partir comme ça.

Sylvie: Écoute, papa! La tante de Marie a loué une villa pour ses enfants et ses petits-enfants mais au dernier moment ils ont dû annuler. **Elle propose que nous y allions**[16] **pour qu'elle ne perde**[17] **pas l'argent** qu'elle a déjà payé. Et elle sera là pour nous surveiller tout le temps.

Père: **C'est dommage que tu n'aies pas bien expliqué**[18] tout ça au début!

Sylvie: Bravo, papa! **C'est dommage que tu ne fasses**[19] **pas toujours attention** à ce qu'on te dit!

10.1 Uses of the subjunctive: general note

○ The tenses you have come across so far (present, future, perfect, imperfect, pluperfect) are in what is called the ***indicative*** mood.

Four of these tenses (present, perfect, imperfect and pluperfect) are also used in what is called the ***subjunctive*** mood.

○ Very broadly speaking, the subjunctive mood is used to talk about something that is one remove from reality, to express an attitude towards an event rather than just to describe the event itself:

Indicative: **Son père est très malade**.
His father is very ill.

Subjunctive: **J'ai peur que son père ne soit très malade.**
I'm afraid that his father is very ill.

○ Probably the best way to cope with the subjunctive is to learn when it is most commonly used.

The subjunctive is used:

i.   after certain conjunctions. For example: **avant que** *(before),* **bien que** and **quoique***(although)*

ii. after any expression of emotion. For example: **je suis content que, je regrette que, cela m'étonne que**...

iii. after impersonal phrases. For example: **il est naturel que, il est rare que..., il vaut mieux que...,** except a few impersonal constructions which express certainty, e.g**. il est évident/clair que..., il est probable que...**

iv. after all expressions of doubt and uncertainty. For example**: je doute que..., je ne crois pas que... je ne suis pas sûr(e) que..., ce n'est pas que...**

v.   after verbs of liking, wishing, preferring, (when you want somebody to do something or you prefer someone to do something). For example**: je n'aime pas** qu'elle sorte toute seule le soir. *(I don't like her going out alone in the evening.)*

vi. in relative clauses which depend on

– a superlative:
C'est le meilleur film que j'aie vu cette année.
It's the best film I've seen this year.

– a negative:

Il n'y a rien qu'on puisse faire pour les aider.
There is nothing you can do to help them.

– a vague or indefinite antecedent:

Je cherche une voiture qui ne soit pas trop chère et que
je puisse utiliser pour les trajets de tous les jours.
*I'm looking for a car which is not too expensive that I can use for
short everyday journeys.*

The car does not yet exist as a single specific car. It is just an
imaginary or hypothetical car. It is simply a kind of car which must
have certain qualities (i.e. it must be inexpensive and suitable for
short everyday journeys).

(See page 188 for more details.)

10.2 The present subjunctive:

○ For regular verbs the stem is formed by removing the **-ent** from the
third person plural (**ils/elles** form) of the present tense.

○ The endings for all verbs (except avoir and être) are:

Je	**–e**	nous	**–ions**
tu	**–es**	vous	**–iez**
il/elle/on	**–e**	ils/elles	**–ent**

○ Look carefully at the examples below:

Infinitive	Ils form present tense	Subjunctive stem	Je form subjunctive
finir	ils finissent	finiss	je finisse
prendre	ils prennent	prenn	je prenne
boire	ils boivent	boiv	je boive
venir	ils viennent	vienn	je vienne
écrire	ils écrivent	écriv	j'écrive

A》 Give the **je** form of the **present subjunctive** of the verbs below.

1	partir	**5**	lire
2	connaître	**6**	attendre
3	dire	**7**	choisir
4	mettre	**8**	voir

O Note that **être** and **avoir** are irregular.

être	**avoir**
je sois	j'aie
tu sois	tu aies
il/elle/on soit	il/elle/on ait
nous soyons	nous ayons
vous soyez	vous ayez
ils/elles soient	ils/elles aient

O A number of other important verbs are irregular. Look at the **je** form of these verbs very carefully.

aller:	j'aille	vouloir:	je veuille
faire:	je fasse	savoir:	je sache
pouvoir:	je puisse	valoir:	je vaille

B》 Without referring to the notes above, complete the following sentences by putting the verb in brackets into the **je** form of the **present subjunctive**. Begin with **Il est essentiel que...** each time.

1   ...(FINIR) mes devoirs.
2   ...(FAIRE) attention en classe.
3   ...(APPRENDRE) les verbes irréguliers.
4   ...(VENIR) en classe régulièrement.
5   ...(ALLER) en France aussi souvent que possible.
6   ...(ÊTRE) toujours à l'heure.
7   ...(CHOISIR) bien mes amis.
8   ...(LIRE) un bon journal.
9   ...(SAVOIR) conjuguer les verbes français.
10 ...(ÉCRIRE) souvent à mon correspondant français.

O A few verbs revert to a 'short' form with nous and vous. This 'short' form stem is the same as that of the present tense (indicative):

aller:	j'aille	but	nous **allions**	vous **alliez**
boire:	je boive	but	nous **buvions**	vous **buviez**
prendre:	je prenne	but	nous **prenions**	vous **preniez**
venir:	je vienne	but	nous **venions**	vous **veniez**
devoir:	je doive	but	nous **devions**	vous **deviez**
mourir:	je meure	but	nous **mourions**	vous **mouriez**
vouloir:	je veuille	but	nous **voulions**	vous **vouliez**

○ The endings of the ***present subjunctive*** are the same for virtually all verbs and are not difficult to learn. The important element to make sure of is the stem and the best way to remember it is by learning the **je** form.

C⟩⟩ Write out the **je** form of the present subjunctive of the following verbs starting with **que**.

1	regarder	6	venir	11	lire
2	finir	7	savoir	12	pouvoir
3	descendre	8	aller	13	conduire
4	boire	9	faire	14	être
5	apprendre	10	écrire	15	avoir

Je regrette que la voiture soit tombée en panne.

10.3 The perfect subjunctive

que tu n'aies pas bien expliqué

○ You need to learn the present subjunctive of **avoir** and **être**. They are used as ***auxiliaries*** along with the ***past participle*** to form the ***perfect subjunctive***:

C'est dommage qu'il **ait manqué** le train.
It's a pity he missed the train.

C'est dommage qu'il **soit arrivé** en retard.
It's a pity he arrived late.

○ The perfect subjunctive is simply the subjunctive version of the perfect indicative:

> ***perfect indicative***:
>
> La voiture est tombée en panne.
> *The car has broken down.*
>
> ***perfect subjunctive***:
>
> Je regrette que la voiture soit tombée en panne.
> *I'm sorry the car has broken down.*

>> Sylvie's mother is talking about her daughter's holiday in the South of France. To make it clearer that she is pleased they had such a good time, add **Je suis contente que...** to the beginning of each of her comments and alter the rest of the sentence appropriately.

1 Elle est allée dans le Midi avec ses amies.
2 Elle a pu passer tout le mois d'août là-bas.
3 Elle n'a pas passé tout l'été à Paris.
4 Elle a profité du beau temps.
5 Elle a appris à faire de la planche à voile.
6 Elles ont toutes passé de bonnes vacances là-bas.
7 Elles se sont très bien entendues avec la tante de Marie.
8 Elles ont réussi à s'adapter si facilement à la vie en commun.

10.4 Uses of the subjunctive: detailed practice

○ A number of ***conjunctions*** are followed by a verb in the subjunctive. The list below needs to be learned thoroughly since other conjunctions do not take the subjunctive.

> **avant que** je prenne une telle décision
> *before I take such a decision*
>
> **bien que** je connaisse bien tes amies
> **quoique je** connaisse bien tes amies
> *although I know your friends well*
>
> **pour que** je sache que tu es en bonne compagnie
> **afin que** je sache que tu es en bonne compagnie
> *so that I know you are in good company*

sans que je sois inquiet tout le temps
without my being worried all the time

pourvu que tu me dises avec qui tu y vas
à condition que tu me dises avec qui tu y vas
provided you tell me who you're going with

jusqu'à ce que tu reviennes
until you come back

de peur que tu n'aies un accident
de crainte que tu n'aies un accident
in case you have an accident

à moins qu'il n'y ait quelqu'un pour vous surveiller
unless there's someone to keep an eye on you

A» Sylvie knows that her parents are very keen to ensure her safety.
Complete what Sylvie says about her parents by putting the verb
in brackets into the correct form.

1 Avant que je ne (SORTIR), ma mère me demande toujours où
   je vais.
2 Bien que mes parents (ÊTRE) assez libéraux, ils ne me
   permettent pas de sortir en semaine.
3 Mes parents m'encouragent à travailler pour que je (POUVOIR)
   réussir à mes examens.
4 Ils me laissent sortir pourvu que je leur (DIRE) où je vais.
5 Ils n'aiment pas que je rentre en voiture de peur que le
   chauffeur ne (ÊTRE) ivre.
6 Je ne peux jamais aller à une boum à moins que mon père ne
   (VENIR) me chercher à minuit.
7 Il ne veut pas que nous fassions du camping sans qu'un adulte
   (ÊTRE) là pour nous surveiller.
8 Je vais parler de la villa tout le temps jusqu'à ce que mon père
   me (PERMETTRE) d'y aller.

B» Sylvie's mother expresses her feelings about the trip to the South
of France. Read what she says and then choose the correct form
of the verb to be used in each sentence. (Try to do this without
consulting the list of conjunctions which take the subjunctive on
page 181.)

1 Puisque je connais/connaisse bien Marie,...
2 Avant que tu ne pars/partes,...

3   Alors que moi, je suis contente que tu y vas/ailles,...
4   Pendant que tu vivras/vives avec nous,...
5   Pour que je sais/sache que tu ne cours pas de risques,...
6   Sans que tu dis/dises à la tante de Marie où tu vas,...
7   Pourvu que ton père est/soit d'accord,...
8   Jusqu'à ce que tu vas/ailles à l'université,...
9   Bien que je ne suis/sois pas contre,...
10   Maintenant que je comprends/comprenne la situation,...

○   **Expressions of emotion + subjunctive** (See pages 158 and 171.)

○   **Impersonal phrases + subjunctive** (See page 176.)

○   All expressions conveying doubt are followed by the subjunctive. Below are a few of the more common expressions.

Je doute que...   Je ne dis pas que...
Je ne crois pas que...   Ce n'est pas que...
Je ne suis pas sûr(e) que...   Croyez-vous que...?
Il est douteux que...

○   It is very important to note that expressions like **je crois que**... and **je suis sûr(e) que**... are followed by a verb in the indicative since no idea of doubt is present. Compare the examples below:

Je crois que mes parents me **permettront** de faire du camping. (INDICATIVE)
I think my parents will let me go camping.

Je ne crois pas que mes parents me **permettent** de faire du camping. (SUBJUNCTIVE)
I don't think my parents will let me go camping.

Je suis sûre que Marie **pourra** venir. (INDICATIVE)
I'm sure Marie will be able to come.

Je ne suis pas sûre que Marie **puisse** venir. (SUBJUNCTIVE)
I'm not sure that Marie will be able to come.

C» Complete the sentences below, using the indicative or the subjunctive as appropriate.

1 Je ne crois pas que mes parents (ÊTRE) prêts à me laisser partir en vacances.

2 Je crois que tu (ÊTRE) trop jeune pour partir en vacances seul.

3 Je suis sûr que tu (S'AMUSER) mieux avec nous.

4 Je ne crois pas que ce (ÊTRE) une bonne idée.

5 Crois-tu que Sylvie (POUVOIR) venir? Je doute que ses parents (ÊTRE) d'accord.

6 Ce n'est pas que mes parents n'(AVOIR) pas confiance en moi, c'est qu'on ne (SAVOIR) jamais ce qui peut arriver.

7 Je ne dis pas que Marie (ÊTRE) inintelligente, mais je sais qu'elle (FAIRE) des bêtises de temps en temps.

8 Je ne crois pas que mon père me (PERMETTRE) de camper.

○ The subjunctive is used with verbs like **vouloir, aimer** and **préférer** when someone wants someone else to do something or likes someone to do this or that. Look carefully at these examples:

Marie veut que Sylvie fasse du camping avec elle.
Marie wants Sylvie to go camping with her.

Les parents de Sylvie n'aiment pas qu'elle sorte en semaine.
Sylvie's parents don't like her going out in the week.

D» Parents are often very demanding. They have a very clear idea of how they would like their children to behave. Rephrase these sentences expressing their views, **using vouloir, aimer, préférer** as indicated.

1 Les parents de Sylvie lui disent toujours de rentrer en taxi.
Les parents de Sylvie veulent toujours qu' ___

2 Ils encouragent Sylvie à sortir avec des jeunes qu'ils connaissent.
Ils préfèrent que Sylvie ___

3 Sylvie a demandé à son père de venir la chercher en voiture.
Sylvie veut que ___

4 Les parents de Sylvie l'encouragent à bien faire son travail scolaire.
Les parents de Sylvie aiment qu'elle ___

5   Les parents conseillent souvent à leurs enfants de ne pas trop
     boire.
     Les parents n'aiment pas que ___

6   Tous les parents veulent des enfants intelligents, beaux et
     sportifs.
     Tous les parents aiment que leurs ___

○   The subjunctive is used in relative clauses which are dependent on:

i.   **a superlative**

     C'est **le meilleur camping que je connaisse**.
     It's the best campsite I know.

ii.   **a negative**:

     Il n'y a rien que je puisse faire pour le faire changer d'avis.
     There is nothing I can do to make him change his mind.

iii. **a hypothetical antecedent**, where the thing being talked
      about exists only in somebody's mind (it is not a concrete
      reality or a specific thing):

     Je cherche un camping qui ne soit pas trop loin de la
     mer et **où il y ait** de bons équipements sportifs.
     *I'm looking for a campsite which isn't too far from the sea and where
     there are good sports facilities.*

The campsite does not exist as a particular place: it is simply an idea
in the speaker's mind. It is a certain kind of campsite that must
have two features: it must be close to the sea and have good sports
facilities. Once a specific campsite has been found, it becomes 'real'
and the relative clause is in the indicative:

J'ai eu de la chance. J'ai trouvé un camping près de Carnac qui n'est
pas loin de la mer et où il y a de bons équipements sportifs.

E》 Use the indicative or subjunctive as appropriate to complete what
Sylvie says.

1   Il n'y a personne qui (POUVOIR) nous surveiller.
2   Je voudrais acheter une voiture qui ne (ÊTRE) pas trop vieille et
     qui (ÊTRE) assez grande pour emmener mes copains au lycée.
3   Au lycée nous avons trouvé cinq filles qui (VOULOIR) aller dans
     le Midi.

4 J'aimerais beaucoup rencontrer un garçon qui (AVOIR) les mêmes goûts que moi en matière de musique.

5 Je ne connais personne qui (ÊTRE) aussi obstiné que mon père.

6 J'ai trouvé quelqu'un qui (POUVOIR) nous emmener dans le Midi en voiture.

7 Je ne veux rien faire qui (FAIRE) de la peine à mes parents.

8 La tante de Marie a loué une villa où il y (AVOIR) de la place pour une dizaine de personnes.

Appendix 1
Prepositions

○ A select list of prepositions and prepositional phrases for AS and A2 levels:

après	*after*
d'après	*according to*
autour de	*around*
aux alentours de (Paris)	*in the area round (Paris)*
avant	*before*
avec	*with*
au bout de (six mois)	*after (six months)*
à cause de	*because of*
chez (les Français)	*in the case of, among*
en ce qui concerne (les jeunes)	*as far as (young people) are concerned*
contre	*against*
à côté de	*beside*
de l'autre côté de	*on the other side of*
au cours (des 30 dernières années)	*over (the last 30 years)*
de crainte de	*for fear of*
au-delà de	*beyond*
en dépit de	*in spite of*
aux dépens de	*at the expense of*
depuis	*since*
derrière	*behind*
dès (le début)	*right from (the beginning)*
au-dessous de (la moyenne)	*below (average)*
au-dessus de (la moyenne)	*above (average)*
au détriment de	*at the expense of*
dont	*including*
en bas de	*at the bottom of*
à l'égard de	*with regard to*
en face de	*opposite*
en haut de	*at the top of*
entre	*between*
envers	*towards*
face à	*faced with*
faute de	*for want of*
grâce à	*thanks to*
hors de	*out of, away from*
jusqu'à	*as far as, until*
jusqu'en (2020)	*until (2020)*
au lieu de	*instead of*
loin de	*far from*
le long de (la rue)	*along (the street)*
tout le long de (l'année)	*throughout (the year)*

lors de	*at the time of, during*
malgré	*in spite of*
en matière de (politique)	*as far as (politics) is concerned*
au milieu de	*in the middle of*
en plein milieu de	*right in the middle of*
au moyen de	*by means of*
par	*by, through*
parmi	*among*
à part	*apart from*
à partir de	*from, starting from*
pendant	*during*
de peur de	*for fear of*
près de (mille francs)	*nearly (1000 francs)*
à propos de	*about, concerning*
quant à	*as for*
en raison de	*on account of*
par rapport à	*in comparison with, in relation to*
sans	*without*
sauf	*except*
au sein de (la famille)	*within (the family)*
selon	*according to*
par suite de	*as a result of*
au sujet de	*about, concerning*
sur	*on, about*
à travers (la France)	*across (France)*
vers	*towards*
vis-à-vis de	*with regard to, towards*
y compris	*including*

Appendix 2   A select list of conjunctions

Linking conjunctions

mais	*but*
au contraire	*on the contrary*
en revanche, par contre	*on the other hand*
pourtant, cependant, néanmoins, toutefois, quand même, tout de même	*however, nevertheless*
car, comme, parce que, puisque	*for, since, because*
étant donné que, vu que	*seeing that*
d'autant plus... que	*all the more so since*
dans la mesure où	*insofar as*
d'ailleurs, de plus, en outre, qui plus est	*besides, moreover*
donc, alors, par conséquent	*and so, therefore*
en fait, en effet, à vrai dire	*in fact*
bien sûr	*of course*
certes	*certainly*
d'abord	*firstly*
puis	*then, secondly*
enfin	*finally*
bref, en résumé	*in short, to sum up*
or	*now (introducing a new element in an argument)*
de toute façon, en tout cas	*in any case*

Other conjunctions

○　The conjunctions marked (s) in the list below are followed by a verb in the **subjunctive** (10.4 p.181) : all the others take the **indicative**.

afin que (s)	*so that, in order that*	même si	*even if*
alors que	*whereas, just when*	(au fur et) à mesure que	*as*
après que	*after*		
aussitôt que	*as soon as*	à peine... que	*hardly/scarcely ... when*
avant que (s)	*before*		
bien que (s)	*although*	pendant que	*while*
chaque fois que	*whenever*	de peur que (s)	*for fear that, in case*
comme si	*as if*	pour que (s)	*so that, in order that*
à condition que (s)	*if only, on condition that*	pourvu que (s)	*provided that, if only*
		quoique (s)	*although*
depuis que	*since*	sans que (s)	*without*
dès que	*as soon as*	de sorte que	*with the result that*
jusqu'au moment où	*until*	tandis que	*while, whereas*
jusqu'à ce que (s)	*until*	tant que	*as long as*
lorsque	*when*		

Appendix 3
The past historic tense

O   You need to be able to recognise this tense, which is used to narrate what happened in the past and is equivalent to the simple past tense in English.

For example, **il se leva** = *he got up*, **il finit** = *he finished*, **il attendit** = *he waited*.

Forms of the past historic

Regular verbs

-er verbs e.g. donner : je donnai, il donna, nous donnâmes, ils donnèrent
-ir verbs e.g. finir : je finis, il finit, nous finîmes, ils finirent
-re verbs e.g. attendre : j'attendis, il attendit, nous attendîmes, ils attendirent

Irregular verbs

All irregular verbs follow one of the patterns below.

i.   **-is** type verbs e.g. prendre : je pris, il prit, nous prîmes, ils prirent
ii. **-us** type verbs e.g. être : je fus, il fut, nous fûmes, ils furent

Here is a list of important irregular verbs.

s'asseoir	je m'assis
avoir	j'eus
boire	je bus
conduire	je conduisis
courir	je courus
croire	je crus
devoir	je dus
dire	je dis
écrire	j'écrivis
éteindre	j'éteignis
être	je fus
faire	je fis
lire	je lus
mettre	je mis
mourir	je mourus
naître	je naquis
pouvoir	je pus
prendre	je pris
recevoir	je reçus
rire	je ris
savoir	je sus
venir	je vins
vivre	je vécus
voir	je vis
vouloir	je voulus
il y a	il y eut

189

Solutions

UNIT 1

1.1

1 Pour aller à la place Grenette? **2** Pour aller au parc Paul-Mistral? **3** Pour aller à l'Hôtel de Ville? **4** Pour aller à l'église Saint-André? **5** Pour aller au stade municipal? **6** Pour aller aux magasins de centre? **7** Pour aller à la vieille ville? **8** Pour aller à l'université? **9** Pour aller aux instituts de géographie alpine et de géologie?

1.2

1 La gare? C'est à 200 mètres de l'hôtel. **2** La piscine? C'est à 50 mètres d'ici, près de la patinoire. **3** Huez? C'est un petit village, à 4 kilomètres environ de l'Alpe-d'Huez. **4** L'hôtel Le Christina? C'est à 5 minutes d'ici.

1.3

1 C'est tout près de la patinoire. **2** C'est tout près de l'héliport. **3** C'est tout près de la piscine. **4** C'est tout près du syndicat d'initiative. **5** C'est tout près des équipements sportifs. **6** C'est tout près de l'école de ski. **7** C'est tout près du téléphérique. **8** C'est tout près des remonte-pentes. **9** C'est tout près de l'arrêt de car. **10** C'est tout près des magasins.

1.4

A

1 En faisant **2** En choisissant **3** En se mettant **4** En commençant **5** En achetant **6** En allant **7** En partageant **8** En prenant

B

1 En sortant **2** En arrivant **3** En allant un peu plus loin **4** En achetant **5** En descendant **6** En voyant le téléphérique

C

1 En prenant **2** En faisant **3** En attendant **4** En finissant **5** En partant

1.5

A

1 Sans écouter **2** en courant **3** Au lieu d'aller **4** dans l'espoir de prendre **5** sans devoir **6** Il a réussi à trouver **7** En voyant **8** sans même ralentir **9** il a fini par y trouver **10** Il a réussi à arriver **11** sans changer **12** En arrivant **13** il a commencé par chercher **14** afin d'y louer **15** Pour s'échauffer **16** il a commencé par descendre **17** il a réussi à descendre

B

Without listening to the hotelier's advice, he ran out of the hotel. Instead of going to the coach station, he looked for the nearest coach stop hoping to be able to catch the coach without having to go all the way to the coach station. He managed to find the right stop. On seeing the coach, he raised his arm but the coach went by without even slowing down. Fortunately, a second coach arrived and in the end he managed to find a seat. He managed to get to l'Alpe-d'Huez in an hour and a quarter without changing coaches.

When he arrived he began by looking for M. Loup's shop in order to hire some skis. To warm up he began by going down several blue runs. Finally he managed to go down a black run without difficulty.

1.6
A
1 en Belgique **2** aux Pays-Bas **3** en France **4** en Allemagne **5** en Espagne **6** au Portugal **7** au Canada **8** aux États-Unis **9** en Amérique du Sud **10** au Mexique **11** au Brésil **12** au Pérou
B
1 d'Amérique du Sud **2** du Chili **3** des États-Unis **4** du Mexique **5** du Brésil **6** d'Argentine **7** du Chili **8** des États-Unis
C
1 France **2** la France **3** la France **4** France **5** France **6** France **7** la France **8** France **9** la France **10** France
D
1 Dunkerque est dans le nord de la France. **2** Dunkerque est à l'est de Calais. **3** La Chartreuse est au nord de Grenoble. **4** Versailles est à l'ouest de Paris. **5** Bordeaux est dans le sud-ouest de la France.

1.7
1 Oui, il y en a trois ou quatre. **2** Oui, j'en ai fait en Suisse et en Autriche. **3** Il y en a qui adorent le ski. **4** Non, je n'en ai pas. Je vais en louer à l'Alpe-d'Huez. **5** Je vais en acheter là-haut. **6** Non merci, j'en ai une dans ma chambre.

1.8
1 en trois jours **2** dans huit jours **3** en quelques heures **4** dans un jour ou deux **5** en trois minutes **6** Dans deux ou trois jours **7** en 45 minutes. **8** en une demi-heure

1.9
1 de **2** – **3** de **4** des **5** de **6** de **7** des **8** de **9** des **10** de **11** – **12** de

UNIT 2

2.1
A
1 savez **2** sais **3** vais **4** faites **5** lis **6** fais **7** connais **8** offre **9** buvez **10** bois **11** voyez **12** vois **13** sors **14** peux **15** vivez **16** vis **17** dois **18** veux **19** ai **20** mets **21** apprends **22** dors **23** crois **24** vis
B
1 font **2** veulent **3** prennent **4** ont **5** sont **6** peuvent **7** connaissent **8** voient **9** vont **10** conduisent **11** viennent **12** doivent **13** savent
C
1 aimons **2** avons **3** sortons **4** faisons **5** lisons **6** dormons **7** prenons **8** mangeons **9** connaissons **10** commençons **11** disons
D
1– Mon ami, Paul, et moi nous retrouvons... **2** Nous nous promenons... **3** Puis nous nous installons... **4** Le patron s'occupe... **5** Nous nous racontons... **6** Tu te rappelles... **7** Tu te souviens... **8** On se dispute... **9** On s'entend bien... **10** Les autres ne s'intéressent pas... **11** Ils s'amusent... **12** Quelquefois ils se moquent de nous... **13** Vous ne vous ennuyez pas... **14** On ne s'ennuie jamais...

2.3
A
1 Il faisait 2 Nous conduisions 3 Ils prenaient 4 Je finissais 5 Nous jouions 6 Elle lisait 7 Elles travaillaient 8 Je mangeais
B
1 travaillais 2 commençais 3 finissais 4 avais 5 mangeais 6 étais 7 sortais
8 lisais 9 prenais 10 faisais 11 mettais 12 allais 13 buvais 14 connaissais
15 disait

2.4
1 peuvent 2 savent 3 savent 4 savent 5 savent 6 peuvent 7 savent 8 peuvent
9 peuvent 10 peuvent 11 savent 12 peuvent 13 savent 14 peuvent 15 peuvent

2.5
1 Le matin 2 L'été 3 du matin 4 du soir 5 L'hiver 6 du soir 7 Le soir/Les soirs
8 Le week-end 9 le dimanche/les dimanches 10 le samedi/les samedis 11 Le samedi soir/Les samedis soirs 12 le dimanche matin/les dimanches matins 13 de l'après-midi

2.6
A
1 La vie était plus dure... on était plus pauvre.
2 Les rues étaient moins encombrées. Le village était plus calme.
3 On était moins pressé.
4 Les gens étaient plus sociables et plus décontractés: ils étaient moins fatigués et moins tendus.
5 Le marché était beaucoup plus animé que maintenant.
B
1 Le bal du samedi soir n'est pas si fréquenté qu'autrefois. 2 Le travail à la ferme n'est pas si dur qu'autrefois. 3 Le village n'est pas si animé le dimanche. 4 Les sentiments de solidarité ne sont pas si forts que par le passé. 5 Les jardins ne sont pas si grands qu'autrefois.

2.7
1 la même école que 2 la même classe que 3 le même travail que 4 les mêmes préoccupations que

2.8
A
1 se rencontraient 2 Ils se disaient bonjour et se serraient la main. 3 ils s'entraidaient 4 Ils s'entendaient 5 ils se voyaient 6 ils se parlaient 7 ils se réunissaient
B
In the old days people in the village met several times a day. They said hello and shook hands. If there were problems, they helped each other out. They got on very well. When they saw each other in the street, they talked for a long time, and in the evenings they met as often as possible.

UNIT 3
3.1
A
1 des 2 des 3 de 4 de 5 de 6 de

B
1 Il y a de nouvelles stations balnéaires mais on trouve aussi de jolis ports de pêche.
2 Il y a de grands campings où de nombreux Anglais passent leurs vacances parce qu'il y a de belles plages tout le long de cette côte.
3 À la campagne, il y a de petites maisons qu'on peut louer à la quinzaine ou au mois.
4 Il y aussi de vieux châteaux qu'on peut visiter.
5 Dans cette région, on peut passer de très bonnes vacances.
C
1 de grands campings 2 de nombreuses familles françaises 3 D'autres estivants
4 de grands hôtels 5 de longues années 6 d'autres 7 de jolis ports de pêche
8 des promenades en mer agréables 9 de bons petits restaurants 10 des fruits de mer délicieux

3.2
A
1 C'est le plus grand port de pêche de la région.
2 C'est la station la plus chère de la région.
3 C'est l'église la plus ancienne de la région.
4 C'est le plus joli village de la région.
5 C'est la station la plus moderne de la région.
6 C'est la plus belle plage de la région.
7 Ce sont les hôtels les plus confortables de la région.
8 Ce sont les campings les plus tranquilles de la région.
B
1 C'est le meilleur restaurant de la ville pour les fruits de mer.
2 C'est la meilleure région de France pour la pêche.
3 Ce sont les meilleurs ports de la région pour la navigation de plaisance.
4 Ce sont les meilleures plages de France pour les enfants.

3.3
1 que j'aie jamais vu 2 que j'aie jamais visité 3 que j'aie jamais goûté 4 que j'aie jamais rencontré 5 que j'aie jamais fait

3.4
A
1 que 2 qui 3 que 4 que 5 qui 6 que 7 qui 8 que
B
1 qu' 2 dont 3 qui 4 dont 5 qui 6 dont 7 que 8 dont

3.5
A
1 tous 2 Toute 3 Tout 4 toutes 5 tous 6 tous 7 Toutes 8 tout 9 toute 10 Tous
11 Tous 12 toute 13 Toute
B
1 Tout le monde 2 Tout 3 tout 4 Tout 5 tous 6 tout le monde 7 tout 8 tout
9 tous 10 tout le monde

3.6
1 de 2 d' 3 des 4 de 5 des 6 d' 7 de 8 d' 9 des 10 de 11 de 12 des

3.7
A
1 ils ont choisi 2 tu as joué 3 j'ai vendu 4 nous avons dîné 5 j'ai acheté 6 elle a attendu 7 nous avons loué 8 vous avez fini

B

1 elle est allée **2** ils sont partis **3** nous sommes arrivé(e)s **4** elles sont descendues **5** elle est montée **6** nous sommes resté(e)s **7** il est tombé **8** ils sont rentrés

C

Cet été, nous sommes allés sur la côte Atlantique. Nous sommes allés dans un camping près des Sables-d'Olonne. Les garçons sont allés avec moi (à la) fin juillet mais mon mari est resté une semaine à Paris. Finalement, il est arrivé le 7 août. Ma sœur est venue aux Sables-d'Olonne vers la fin du mois. Elle est allée à l'hôtel et nous sommes tous sortis ensemble plusieurs fois. Enfin, nous sommes tous rentrés/retournés à Paris à la fin août/du mois d'août.

D

1 je me suis levé(e) **2** il s'est baigné **3** nous nous sommes promené(e)s **4** ils se sont amusés **5** elle s'est reposée **6** vous vous êtes couché(e)(s)

E

1 Nous sommes allés **2** nous avons fait **3** Nous sommes restés **4** Les enfants se sont amusés **5** Ils se sont baignés **6** ils sont allés **7** ils ont essayé **8** Sophie et Anne se sont promenées à cheval **9** Nous avons mangé **10** nous avons dîné

3.8

1 Georges? Il vient de sortir.
2 ...ils viennent d'acheter une villa...
3 Nous venons de dîner...
4 Je viens de leur téléphoner.
5 Je viens de rentrer de vacances.

3.9

1 nous avons passé **2** on allait **3** on a fait **4** nous faisions **5** nous avons décidé **6** Nous sommes montés **7** il y avait **8** nous avons visité **9** nous nous sommes promenés **10** nous sommes repartis **11** nous approchions **12** nous avons vu **13** se trouvait notre camping **14** Nous avons continué **15** nous avons dû **16** la route était **17** Tous les arbres brûlaient **18** On nous a dit **19** les pompiers essayaient **20** des avions déversaient **21** le vent soufflait **22** le feu se propageait **23** On nous a conseillé **24** Nous étions **25** nous avons décidé **26** nous sommes rentrés **27** tous les arbres étaient calcinés **28** on avait **29** le camping risquait **30** nous avons décidé

UNIT 4

4.1

A

1 tu travailleras **2** il prendra **3** nous trouverons **4** elles finiront **5** elle passera **6** je payerai **7** vous parlerez **8** ils gagneront

B

1 J'irai **2** Je pourrai **3** Je travaillerai **4** Je ferai **5** Je verrai **6** Je sortirai **7** J'apprendrai **8** J'achèterai **9** J'aurai **10** je devrai **11** Je reviendrai **12** Je rentrerai

4.2

A

1 Quand j'arriverai à Brighton, j'irai/je resterai chez Nick.
2 Quand j'aurai un job/un emploi, je chercherai une chambre.
3 Quand je sortirai le week-end, je pourrrai parler anglais avec les amis/copains de Nick.

B

1 Si je passe **2** Quand j'aurai **3** Quand je serai **4** Si je parle **5** Si tout marche
6 Quand je me débrouillerai **7** Quand Nick et ses amis parleront **8** Si j'apprends
9 Quand j'habiterai **10** Si j'ai

4.3
A

1 ...j'aurai fini mes études
2 ...je me serai installé à Londres
3 ...j'aurai appris à parler anglais
4 ...je me serai marié
5 ...ma femme et moi aurons gagné beaucoup d'argent
6 ...nous serons allés travailler aux Etats-Unis
7 ...la vie sera devenue trè facile

4.4
1 à **2** de **3** à **4** à **5** à **6** de **7** à **8** à **9** de **10** à

4.5
B

1 d' **2** d' **3** – **4** de **5** – **6** de **7** à **8** à **9** à **10** – **11** – **12** – **13** à **14** – **15** à **16** –
17 de **18** à **19** – **20** de **21** de **22** à **23** à **24** à **25** de

4.6
1 Où vas-tu habiter en Grande-Bretagne?
   Où est-ce que tu vas habiter en Grande-Bretagne?
2 Combien d'argent espères-tu gagner?
   Combien d'argent est-ce que tu espères gagner?
3 Quand vas-tu rentrer en France?
   Quand est-ce que tu vas rentrer en France?
4 Quand Pierre part-il pour Brighton?
   Quand est-ce que Pierre part pour Brighton?
5 Comment va-t-il voyager?
   Comment est-ce qu'il va voyager?
6 La famille de Nick peut-elle héberger Pierre longtemps?
   Est-ce que la famille de Nick peut héberger Pierre longtemps?
7 Quelle sorte de job veux-tu trouver?
   Quelle sorte de job est-ce que tu veux trouver?
8 Pierre parle-t-il bien le français?
   Est-ce que Pierre parle bien le français?

4.7
A

1 Qu'est-ce que **2** ce que **3** qu'est-ce qui **4** ce qu' **5** Qu'est-ce que **6** Ce qui
7 ce que **8** ce qui
B

1 ce qui **2** Ce qui **3** quoi **4** Quelle **5** Qu'est-ce que **6** qu'est-ce qu' **7** ce que
8 quoi **9** ce que **10** ce que **11** ce qui

4.8
1 cela **2** C' **3** cela **4** ce **5** Cela **6** C' **7** ce **8** cela **9** cela **10** cela

4.9

A

1 fils unique 2 programmeur 3 lycéen 4 comptable 5 plombier 6 serveur
7 coiffeuse 8 chauffeur de taxi 9 professeur 10 chômeur

B

1 Jérôme veut devenir homme d'affaires. 2 Il est toujours lycéen/étudiant. 3 Il
travaille comme serveur pendant les vacances. 4 Son père est professeur. 5 Sa mère
est journaliste. 6 Sa sœur a déjà trouvé un emploi. Elle travaille comme comptable.

UNIT 5

5.1

A

La monitrice a demandé à son élève...

1 ...d'attendre le feu vert.
2 ...d'utiliser le rétroviseur plus souvent.
3 ...de ralentir en approchant du rond-point
4 ... de boucler la ceinture de sécurité.
5 ...de faire attention tout le temps.
6 ...de penser aux autres automobilistes.
7 ...de conduire plus lentement.
8 ...de prendre moins de risques.

B

1 Martin a demandé à son père d'acheter une vieille bagnole.
2 La monitrice a conseillé à Martin de vérifier l'état des pneus.
3 On a dit à Martin de rester à l'hôpital.
4 On a permis aux autres jeunes de rentrer chez eux.
5 Le père de Florence a ordonné à la jeune fille de ne plus sortir avec Martin.
6 Le garagiste a dit au jeune homme de faire réparer les dégâts aussi vite que possible.

C

1 On lui conseille de ne pas démarrer trop brusquement.
2 On lui dit de conduire avec prudence.
3 Souvent les parents leur permettent de conduire la voiture familiale.
4 On leur demande souvent d'acheter une voiture d'occasion.

5.2

1 J'ai aidé beaucoup de jeunes à obtenir le permis de conduire.
2 Je ne permets pas à mes élèves de fumer.
3 J'encourage mes élèves à utiliser le rétroviseur tout le temps.
4 Au début vous ne devriez pas inviter vos copains à monter dans votre voiture.
5 On conseille à tous les jeunes de conduire avec prudence.
6 On oblige tous les débutants à rouler à moins de 90 kilomètres à l'heure.

5.3

A

1 Freine plus doucement! 2 Conduis avec prudence! 3 Pense aux autres
automobilistes! 4 Change de vitesse plus tôt! 5 Démarrons maintenant!
6 Prenons la deuxième à gauche! 7 Faisons cette manoeuvre encore une fois!
8 Finissons maintenant! 9 Lisez le code de la route très attentivement! 10 Faites
attention tout le temps! 11 Ralentissez avant d'arriver à un rond-point! 12 Partez
toujours à temps!

B

1 Martin, dépêche-toi! **2** Monte dans la voiture! **3** Installe-toi confortablement!
4 Vérifie le frein à main et le levier de vitesse! **5** Calme-toi! **6** Prépare-toi bien pour l'épreuve! **7** Rappelle-toi tous mes conseils!

C

1 Ne vous mettez pas au milieu de la chaussée! **2** Ne vous approchez pas trop des autres véhicules! **3** Ne vous arrêtez pas trop près du trottoir! **4** Ne vous fâchez pas! **5** Ne nous disputons pas!

D

1 Ne t'amuse pas à regarder ce qui se passe dans la rue! **2** Ne t'occupe pas des erreurs des autres automobilistes! **3** Ne te trompe pas de vitesse!

5.4

A

1 Après avoir changé la roue, ils se sont remis en route.
2 Après avoir réussi à l'examen du code de la route, on peut passer le permis de conduire.
3 Après avoir appris à conduire, les jeunes veulent acheter une voiture à eux.
4 Après que la voiture était tombée en panne plusieurs fois, on a décidé de la vendre.
5 Après ma première leçon, j'ai pensé que je n'obtiendrais jamais mon permis de conduire.
6 Après que Martin avait donné son nom et son adresse, le policier lui a permis de partir.
7 Après avoir pris un café et après s'être reposé un peu, il a pu continuer son chemin.
8 Après avoir réussi au permis de conduire, il a demandé à ses parents de lui acheter une voiture.

B

1 Après s'être installée...
2 Après avoir vérifié...
3 Après avoir mis...
4 Après s'être assurée...
5 Après avoir conduit...
6 Après s'être arrêtés...
7 Après avoir écouté...
8 Après avoir pris...
9 Après m'être habitué(e)...
10 Après être sorti...

5.5

1 avant de **2** Avant qu' **3** Avant de **4** Avant d' **5** avant **6** avant qu' **7** avant de
8 Avant de

5.6

1 Tu devrais regarder dans ton rétroviseur.
2 Vous ne devriez pas changer de voie sans utiliser le clignotant.
3 Tu aurais dû t'arrêter au feu rouge.
4 On aurait dû acheter une bonne carte routière.
5 Vous devriez toujours boucler votre ceinture avant de partir.
6 On ne devrait jamais rouler vite quand les routes sont mouillées.
7 Vous n'auriez pas dû traverser le carrefour sans regarder à droite ni à gauche.
8 Vous n'auriez pas dû brûler les feux.

5.7

A

1 C'est la dernière fois que je sors avec lui!

2 Le dernier garage avait les pièces dont nous avions besoin.

3 J'ai passé mon permis de conduire la dernière semaine des vacances de Pâques.

4 Il a acheté une nouvelle voiture le mois dernier.

5 Dans les cinq dernières années, ils ont sorti trois nouveaux modèles.

B

1 La semaine prochaine, j'espère acheter une nouvelle voiture.

2 Dans les 20 prochaines années, beaucoup de Français vont acheter une voiture.

3 Lundi prochain, j'irai au lycée en voiture pour la première fois.

5.8

1 Il 2 C' 3 c' 4 Il 5 Il 6 c' 7 c' 8 c' 9 Il 10 c' 11 c' 12 c'

5.9

A

1 Généralement 2 prudemment 3 lentement 4 doucement 5 Normalement
6 attentivement 7 dangereusement 8 Fréquemment 9 absolument 10 vraiment
11 bien 12 constamment 13 adroitement 14 mal

B

1 avec colère 2 d'une façon décisive/de façon décisive* 3 avec patience 4 d'une
façon convaincante/de façon convaincante* 5 avec amour 6 d'une façon
impressionnante/de façon impressionnante* 7 avec sympathie 8 d'une façon
efficace/de façon efficace*

*The word façon can be replaced by manière.

5.11

J'ai fait changer les freins.

J'ai fait remplacer les phares.

J'ai fait réparer le toit.

J'ai fait repeindre la carrosserie.

J'ai fait recouvrir les sièges.

J'ai fait installer un système CD.

5.11

1 – 2 – 3 à 4 à 5 à 6 à; – 7 à 8 –; à 9 d' 10 de 11 de 12 de 13 de 14 –; –
15 de; d' 16 d' 17 à

UNIT 6

6.1

A

1 Quelle bonne idée! 2 Quelle bonne surprise! 3 Quel homme sympathique!
4 Quelle belle journée!

B

1 Quelle bonne nouvelle! 2 Quel enfant intelligent! 3 Quelle jolie robe! 4 Quel bel
appartement! 5 Quel costume élégant! 6 Quelle belle ville! 7 Quelles filles
charmantes! 8 Quels beaux magasins!

6.2

1 les 2 les 3 la 4 le 5 l' 6 le 7 le 8 les

6.3
– Thomas t'emmène souvent au théâtre?
– Oui, de temps en temps. Il me contacte au cours de la journée pour voir si une pièce m'intéresse. Puis il vient me chercher au bureau vers six heures.
– On voit bien que Thomas te gâte! Il doit t'aimer beaucoup!
– Et tes amis, ils ne t'invitent jamais à aller au théâtre?
– Non, ils m'invitent à aller au cinéma ou au restaurant mais ils refusent de m'accompagner au théâtre. Ils (me) demandent tout le temps pourquoi le théâtre m'intéresse et ils refusent de me croire quand je dis qu'un vrai spectacle me passionne beaucoup plus qu'un film.
– Alors moi, je t'invite à venir avec nous la prochaine fois. Thomas sera très content de t'emmener au théâtre, je te le promets!

6.4
A
1 Je leur parle de toutes sortes de choses. **2** Je lui ai montré les articles. **3** Je veux leur donner un cadeau. **4** Je vais leur téléphoner ce soir. **5** Dis-lui bonjour de ma part! **6** Demande-lui de te donner un jour de congé!
B
1 Je leur ai offert les billets. **2** Je lui ai demandé de me téléphoner/de me donner un coup de téléphone. **3** Je leur ai dit que j'étais occupé(e). **4** Je lui ai donné mon numéro de téléphone.

6.5
1 Oui, j'en ai écrit plusieurs. **2** J'y vais deux fois par mois en moyenne. **3** J'y habite depuis deux mois seulement. **4** Oui, il en a deux. **5** Il y en a une dizaine. **6** Je vais y rester encore plusieurs mois. **7** J'espère en écrire six. **8** J'y ai passé un an et demi.

6.6
A
1 J'y travaille comme secrétaire. **2** Invite-les à venir! **3** Je lui ai dit que je serais un peu en retard. **4** Demande-lui de me téléphoner! **5** Je la connais depuis longtemps. **6** Regarde-les! **7** J'y ai passé un an. **8** Allons-y vendredi soir! **9** Dis-leur de parler français! **10** Habituellement, je leur parle en anglais.
B
1 Tu dois lui téléphoner ce soir. **2** Tu dois leur montrer ce que tu as écrit. **3** Tu dois m'expliquer exactement ce que tu veux faire. **4** Tu dois lui demander de te donner quelques jours de congé. **5** Tu dois me donner ta nouvelle adresse. **6** Tu dois leur dire que tu veux rester à Paris.
C
– Bonjour, madame. Les clefs de l'appartement de Mlle Prévost, vous pouvez me les donner?
– Les clefs? Je peux vous en donner une mais il y en a trois.
– Vous devez m'en donner au moins deux puisque nous serons deux à y habiter.
– Deux?
– Mais oui, Mlle Prévost ne vous l'a pas dit? Mon fiancé et moi. La deuxième clef, je vais la lui donner.
– Alors je peux vous en donner deux. Et le loyer, vous allez me le verser maintenant?
– Non. Mlle Prévost ne vous l'a pas dit? Je vais le lui envoyer le premier du mois.

– Ah bon.
– Et les clefs, madame, vous allez me les chercher? Je suis pressée.
– Mais oui, madame. Tout de suite.

6.7
1 eux **2** moi **3** lui **4** nous **5** eux **6** toi **7** elle **8** eux

6.8
1 Moi, j'aime beaucoup Paris mais lui, il préfère Bruxelles.
2 Nous, nous adorons le cinéma mais eux, ils préfèrent le théâtre.
3 Moi, je comprends assez bien l'anglais mais toi, tu le parles très bien aussi.
4 Elle, elle est toujours très chic mais moi, j'aime porter des vêtements décontractés le weekend.
5 Toi, tu veux toujours dîner au restaurant. Moi, je préfère manger ici.
6 Nous, nous utilisons le métro autant que possible mais eux, ils vont partout en taxi.

6.9
1 J'ai quelque chose d'important à te dire. **2** J'ai beaucoup de travail à faire ce soir. **3** J'ai le dîner à préparer. **4** J'ai des articles sur le nouveau Paris à écrire. **5** J'ai deux personnes à interviewer. **6** Je n'ai rien à faire vendredi soir. **7** Tu veux quelque chose à boire? **8** Tu veux que je prépare quelque chose à manger?

6.10
A
1 mon salaire **2** ma feuille de paie **3** mon compte en banque **4** mes économies **5** ma carte de crédit **6** mon carnet de chèques **7** mes dépenses **8** mon portefeuille
B
1 Mon **2** mon **3** mon **4** mes **5** mon **6** mon **7** mes **8** mon **9** mon **10** mes **11** mon
C
1 son **2** son **3** son **4** son **5** ses **6** ses **7** son **8** son **9** son **10** son **11** ses **12** ses
D
1 vos **2** nos **3** Nos **4** notre **5** nos **6** vos **7** nos **8** votre **9** vos **10** nos **11** nos **12** nos
E
1 leurs **2** Leur **3** leur **4** leurs **5** leurs **6** leurs **7** Leur **8** leurs **9** leur **10** leurs **11** leur **12** leurs **13** leur **14** leur
F
1 Beaucoup de Parisiens laissent leur voiture dans la rue.
2 Beaucoup de Français aiment que leur femme soit à la maison quand ils rentrent!
3 Beaucoup d'enfants font leur lit pour aider leurs parents.
4 Très peu de gens ont le temps de ranger leur maison avant de sortir le matin.

6.11
1 ...que le nôtre
2 ...que la mienne
3 ...que le vôtre
4 ...que le mien
5 ...que les leurs
6 ...que les tiens
7 ...que la leur
8 ...que le sien

6.12
1 vieille **2** ancienne **3** gentille **4** douce **5** professionnelle **6** active **7** agressive
8 sèche **9** fausse **10** longue **11** malheureuse **12** dernière **13** vieille **14** sportive
15 grosse **16** longues **17** inquiète **18** naturelle **19** folle **20** nouvelle **21** active
22 essentielle **23** ancienne

6.13
1 nouvelle **2** nouvel **3** bel **4** nouvel **5** vieil **6** vieux **7** beaux vieux **8** vieilles
9 belles **10** nouveaux **11** nouvel **12** nouvelle

6.14
A
1 depuis **2** pendant **3** depuis **4** pendant **5** depuis **6** pour (pendant) **7** pendant
8 pour (pendant)
B
1 connaît **2** est **3** travaille **4** habite **5** étudie **6** apprend
C
1 Julie and Sophie have known each other for nearly two years.
2 She has been in Paris for two months.
3 She has been working for M. Ricard for six weeks.
4 She has been living in Françoise's house for two months.
5 She has been studying French for a long time.
6 She has been learning Italian for more than a year.

6.15
1 C'est une fille très sportive. **2** C'est un garçon trè intelligent. **3** C'est un homme
travailleur. **4** C'est une femme très énergique.

UNIT 7
7.1
A
1 de **2** de **3** du **4** du **5** de **6** de **7** des **8** de **9** de la **10** de **11** de **12** de
B
1 des **2** de **3** une **4** un **5** de **6** un **7** d' **8** un **9** de **10** de **11** des **12** de **13** un
14 un **15** des **16** d'

7.2
1 La plupart **2** plusieurs/certains/quelques-uns **3** beaucoup **4** Certains/Quelques-
uns **5** beaucoup **6** la plupart **7** Quelques/Certaines **8** plusieurs **9** Certains
10 plusieurs **11** la plupart **12** Certains **13** La plupart **14** beaucoup

7.3
1 Nous avons trop de travail pour repeindre l'appartement.
2 Les enfants sont trop jeunes pour aller à l'école tout seuls.
3 Nous sommes trop loin des magasins pour y aller à pied.
4 Nous n'avons pas assez d'argent pour louer un appartement dans Paris.
5 Nous habitons trop loin de Paris pour y aller le soir.
6 Nous ne sommes pas assez riches pour acheter une maison en banlieue.

7.4
1 J'habiterais **2** J'achèterais **3** J'apprendrais **4** Je sortirais **5** Je profiterais **6** Je ferais
7 Je ne devrais pas **8** Je pourrais **9** J'irais **10** Je verrais **11** J'aurais **12** Je serais

7.5
A
1 Si je travaillais à Paris 2 Si nous louons 3 Si les enfants avaient 4 si le loyer était moins élevé 5 si le propriétaire accepte 6 Si nous habitions ici
B
1 nous essayerons d'acheter une maison en banlieue 2 si les loyers étaient moins élevés 3 si l'immeuble avait un ascenseur 4 Si nous louons

7.6
1 Cette 2 Ces 3 Cette 4 Ces 5 Ce 6 Cette 7 Cette 8 ces 9 cet 10 cet 11 ce
12 Cet

7.7
A
1 Celle 2 Ceux 3 Celui 4 Celui 5 Celles 6 Ceux
B
1 Celui 2 Cela 3 Celle 4 cela 5 cela 6 Celui

7.8
1 Quelles 2 Lequel 3 Laquelle 4 Quelle 5 Quels 6 Lequel

UNIT 8
8.1
A
1 avait servi 2 avait été 3 avait coûté 4 avaient dû 5 avait espéré 6 avait très mal fait 7 n'avaient pas mangé 8 étaient allés 9 avait recommandé 10 avaient passé
B
1 était allé 2 avait pris 3 avait préparé 4 avait servi 5 avait fait 6 avait choisi
7 avait été 8 avait mangé 9 avait dîné 10 n'avait pas inventé

8.2
1 M. Mermet aurait choisi...
   Cela aurait coûté...
   On aurait mieux mangé...
2 Mme Mermet aurait préparé...
   Elle aurait acheté...
3 'Nous aurions mieux fait...'
4 'J'aurais préféré manger...
   Je serais allé...'
5 Lui et son ami seraient sortis...
   Ils se seraient bien amusés...

8.3
1 bonne 2 bien 3 bon 4 mauvais 5 mauvais 6 mauvaise 7 mal 8 mauvais 9 mal
10 mal 11 bien 12 bonne 13 mauvais 14 bien 15 bien 16 bons

8.4
1 meilleurs 2 mieux 3 meilleurs 4 mieux 5 meilleurs 6 meilleurs 7 mieux
8 meilleurs 9 mieux 10 mieux 11 meilleurs 12 meilleurs 13 mieux 14 meilleure

8.5
1 son 2 ses 3 soi 4 son 5 vous 6 soi 7 son 8 sa 9 ses 10 soi 11 son 12 sa
13 soi 14 son

8.6
1 nous 2 nous 3 vous 4 vous 5 t' 6 m' 7 s' 8 te

8.7
1 qu'on fasse 2 que la cuisine traditionnelle ne soit plus 3 que tant de gens aillent 4 que tout le monde choisisse 5 que les gens sortent 6 que les jeunes ne sachent pas 7 que les Français prennent 8 que toute la famille ait

8.8
1 Le garçon a donné le menu et la carte des vins à la famille Mermet/aux Mermet.
2 Le garçon a donné une petite portion de frites à Michel.
3 Il a offert un autre verre de vin à M. Mermet.
4 M. Mermet a montré l'addition au garçon.
5 Il n'a pas donné de pourboire au garçon.
6 Beaucoup de restaurants offrent un bon choix de plats au client.
7 Mme Mermet a donné de l'argent à son fils pour acheter un hamburger.
8 M. Mermet a envoyé une lettre à la Chambre de Commerce.

8.9
A
1 Je n'ai jamais mangé un tel repas! 2 Je n'ai jamais payé une telle addition! 3 Je n'ai jamais goûté une telle sauce!
B
1 Je n'ai jamais rencontré un garçon si maladroit! 2 Je n'ai jamais passé une soirée si désagréable! 3 On ne m'a jamais servi une si petite portion!

8.10
1 Rien n'est moins sain qu'un hamburger.
2 Personne n'est si désagréable qu'un serveur maladroit.
3 Personne ne cuisine mieux que ma femme.
4 Rien n'est plus satisfaisant qu'un plat traditionnel.
5 Rien n'attire les jeunes autant qu'un Big Mac.
6 Personne ne mange plus mal qu'un adolescent américain.

8.11
A
1 J'aime manger quelque chose d'exotique.
2 Quelquefois on veut impressionner quelqu'un d'important.
3 Je préfère quelque chose de simple et de savoureux.
B
1 Il n'y a rien de plus agréable qu'un dîner entre amis.
2 Il n'y a personne de si désagréable qu'un serveur inattentif et maladroit.
3 Il n'y a rien de moins appétissant qu'un hamburger graisseux.

8.12
A
1 M. Mermet a dit qu'il y avait...
2 Le serveur a répliqué que ce n'était pas possible.
3 M. Mermet a ajouté qu'ils avaient pris...
4 Le serveur a avoué que c'était vrai.
5 Il a ajouté qu'il allait corriger...
6 Mme Mermet a noté qu'il avait trop bu.
7 Elle a expliqué qu'il avait oublié d'apporter les verres.

B
1 'Un de mes collègues a recommandé le restaurant' a dit M. Mermet.
2 'Je me suis vraiment trompé' a-t-il ajouté.
3 'Le serveur a fait plusieurs erreurs' a expliqué Mme Mermet.
4 'Il a trop bu' a-t-elle dit.
5 'J'ai déjà mangé à midi' ai-je dit.
6 'J'ai déjeuné dans la cantine' ai-je ajouté.
7 'Pourquoi as-tu choisi ce restaurant?' a demandé Michel.
8 'Moi, je préfère le fast-food' a-t-il dit.

UNIT 9
9.1
A
1 Dans les années 60 et 70, toutes sortes de mesures ont été prises pour réglementer la circulation automobile à Paris.
2 Certaines rues ont été mises en sens unique.
3 Des zones à stationnement limité ont été créées.
4 Des parcmètres ont été installés
5 et des contractuels ont été embauchés pour faire observer les règlements.
6 Ces mesures ont été acceptées à contre-coeur par l'automobiliste parisien.
7 En même temps, des efforts on été faits pour rendre sa vie plus facile.
8 De nombreux parkings souterrains ont été aménagés
9 et de grands travaux routiers ont été entrepris.
10 Une voie express a été créée le long de la rive droite de la Seine
11 et, en 1970, le Boulevard Périphérique a été mis en service.
12 De plus, de nombreuses autoroutes ont été construites pour améliorer les liaisons routières avec le reste de la France.

B
During the sixties and seventies all sorts of steps were taken to regulate car traffic in Paris. Some streets were made into one-way streets. Restricted parking zones were created. Parking meters were installed and traffic wardens were employed to enforce the rules. Parisian motorists were reluctant to accept these measures. At the same time efforts were made to make their life easier. Several underground car parks were built, and many road works were carried out. A motorway was built along the right bank of the Seine and in 1970 the Parisian ring road was put into service. In addition, a lot of motorways were built to improve road links with the rest of France.

C
1 Quand on a offert son nouvel emploi à Pierre, on lui a donné une voiture plus rapide.
2 On lui permettait de l'utiliser le week-end aussi.
3 On lui demandait souvent d'emmener/de ramener des collègues à Paris.
4 Ce jour-là, on lui a conseillé de partir de bonne heure/tôt parce qu'il y avait du brouillard sur l'autoroute.

9.2
1 Sa femme n'est jamais venue à l'hôpital. 2 Il n'a plus acheté de voiture. 3 Il n'a accusé personne d'avoir causé l'accident. 4 Il n'a jamais essayé d'expliquer l'accident. 5 Il n'a rien fait pour aider les enfants de ses collègues. 6 Il n'a critiqué personne. 7 Il n'a rien fait pour se remettre en forme. 8 Il n'est allé nulle part pour se changer les idées.

9.3
1 Peut-être la voiture a-t-elle dérapé sur le verglas.
 Peut-être que la voiture a dérapé sur le verglas.
 La voiture a peut-être dérapé sur le verglas.
2 Peut-être Pierre était-il un peu fatigué.
 Peut-être que Pierre était un peu fatigué.
 Pierre était peut-être un peu fatigué.
3 Peut-être y avait-il du brouillard sur l'autoroute.
 Peut-être qu'il y avait du brouillard sur l'autoroute.
 Il y avait peut-être du brouillard sur l'autoroute.

9.4
1 En hiver, le brouillard rend les autoroutes très dangereuses.
2 La possession d'une voiture rend la vie plus facile.
3 Mais les voitures rendent tout le monde très paresseux.
4 Quelquefois en ville la circulation rend l'air irrespirable.
5 Les mauvais conducteurs rendent la vie des autres insupportable.
6 Les limitations de vitesse rendent les routes plus sûres.

9.5
1 soit 2 veuille 3 va 4 fasse 5 sache 6 devienne 7 pourra 8 dise

9.6
1 – 2 à 3 de 4 à 5 à 6 de 7 de 8 –; de 9 de 10 à 11 à 12 de 13 d' 14 de
15 de 16 de

UNIT 10

Introductory dialogue. Why the subjunctive is used.
1 After verbs of wishing, liking, preferring 2 After expression of doubt 3 After verb
of wishing etc. 4 After conjunction: avant que 5 After verb of wishing etc.
6 After verb of wishing etc. 7 After verb of wishing etc. 8 After conjunction:
jusqu'à ce que 9 After verb of wishing etc. 10 After conjunction: sans que 11After
indefinite antecedent: quelqu'un 12 After expression of emotion 13 After
impersonal phrase 14 After an indefinite antecedent: une autre solution 15 After
conjunction: avant que 16 After verb of wishing etc. 17 After conjunction: pour
que 18 After expression of emotion/impersonal phrase 19 After expression of
emotion/impersonal phrase

10.2
A
1 que je parte 2 que je connaisse 3 que je dise 4 que je mette 5 que je lise
6 que j'attende 7 que je choisisse 8 que je voie
B
Il est essentiel...
1 que je finisse mes devoirs. 2 que je fasse attention en classe. 3 que j'apprenne
les verbes irréguliers. 4 que je vienne en classe régulièrement. 5 que j'aille en
France aussi souvent que possible. 6 que je sois toujours à l'heure. 7 que je
choisisse bien mes amis. 8 que je lise un bon journal. 9 que je sache conjuguer
les verbes français. 10 que j'écrive souvent à mon correspondant français.

C

1 que je regarde **2** que je finisse **3** que je descende **4** que je boive **5** que j'apprenne
6 que je vienne **7** que je sache **8** que j'aille **9** que je fasse **10** que j'écrive **11** que je
lise **12** que je puisse **13** que je conduise **14** que je sois **15** que j'aie

10.3

Je suis contente...
1 qu'elle soit allée dans le Midi avec ses amies.
2 qu'elle ait pu passer tout le mois d'août là-bas.
3 qu'elle n'ait pas passé tout l'été à Paris.
4 qu'elle ait profité du beau temps.
5 qu'elle ait appris à faire de la planche à voile.
6 qu'elles aient toutes passé de bonnes vacances là-bas.
7 qu'elles se soient très bien entendues avec la tante de Marie.
8 qu'elles aient réussi à s'adapter si facilement à la vie en commun.

10.4

A
1 sorte **2** soient **3** puisse **4** dise **5** soit **6** vienne **7** soit **8** permette
B
1 connais **2** partes **3** ailles **4** vivras **5** sache **6** dises **7** soit **8** ailles **9** sois
10 comprends
C
1 soient **2** es **3** t'amuseras **4** soit **5** puisse; soient **6** aient; sait **7** soit; fait
8 permette
D
1 Les parents de Sylvie veulent toujours qu'elle rentre en taxi.
2 Ils préfèrent que Sylvie sorte avec des jeunes qu'ils connaissent.
3 Sylvie veut que son père vienne la chercher en voiture.
4 Les parents de Sylvie aiment qu'elle fasse bien son travail scolaire.
5 Les parents n'aiment pas que leurs enfants boivent trop.
6 Tous les parents veulent que leurs enfants soient intelligents, beaux et sportifs.
E
1 puisse **2** soit; soit **3** veulent **4** ait **5** soit **6** peut **7** fasse **8** a

Index

Note: Where a phrase appears in italics, this is given as an example of the structure listed.

A

à with adjectives + infinitive **4.4**
à with distances **1.2**
à with nouns (à la, à l', au, aux) **1.1**
à : verbs + à + infinitive **5.12**
à condition que + subjunctive **10.4**
adjectives (irregular) **6.13**
adjectives (agreement) **6.12**
adjectives + à + infinitive **4.4**
adjectives + de + infinitive **4.4**
adverbs (regular and irregular formation) **5.9**
adverbs (comparative and superlative forms) **5.10**
adverbial phrases (*avec un plaisir évident, de façon spectaculaire*) **5.9**
afin que + subjunctive **10.4**
after + noun **5.4**
after + verb (après que) **5.4**
after + verb (après avoir/être + past participle) **5.4**
a lot of (beaucoup de) **3.6**
all + nouns (tout, toute, tous, toutes) **3.5**
à moins que + subjunctive **10.4**
après + noun (*après la boum*) **5.4**
après + verb (après que) **5.4**
après + verb (après avoir/être + past participle) **5.4**
as...as (aussi...que) **2.6**
as : the same as (le même que) **2.7**
ask someone to do something (demander à quelqu'un de faire quelque chose) **5.1**
assez + adjective **7.3**
assez de + noun **7.3**
assez...pour + infinitive **7.3**
au, aux + countries **1.6**
(j) aurais dû (faire) – I ought to have (done) **5.6**
aussi...que **2.6**
avant + noun **5.5**
avant de + infinitive **5.5**
avant que + subjunctive **5.5**

B

bad, badly **8.3**
beau, bel belle **6.13**
beaucoup de + noun **3.6**
before **5.5**
better (meilleur, mieux) **8.4**
bien que + subjunctive **10.4**

bon contrasted with bien 8.3
by doing something (en + present participle) 1.4

C

can (savoir or pouvoir?) 2.4
ce or cela? 4.8
ce, cet, cette, ces 7.6
cela or ce? 4.8
celui, celle, ceux, celles 7.7
ce qui, ce que 4.7
certains (contrasted with quelques) 7.2
c'est or il est? 5.8
c'est, ce sont (with people or things) 6.15
chaque 3.5
command forms 5.3
comparative adjectives 2.7; 2.6
comparative adverbs 5.10
conditional tense 7.4
conditional perfect tense 8.2
conjunctions **Appendix 2**
conjunctions + subjunctive 10.4
countries 1.6

D

dans + expressions of time 1.8
dans + place (*dans le sud-est de la France*) 1.6
de after a negative 7.1
de after a superlative 3.2
de after expressions of quantity 3.6; 7.1
de + adjective + noun 3.1
de + article + noun 1.3
de + feminine countries 1.6
de + infinitive after an adjective 4.4
de + infinitive after a verb 5.12; 9.6
demonstrative articles 7.6
demonstrative pronouns 7.7
dependent infinitives 5.11
depuis contrasted with pendant and pour 6.14
dernier (position of) 5.7
des or de? 3.1
des or les? 7.2
des + plural countries 1.6
des after la plupart 3.6; 7.2
devoir: *je devrais (faire)*, *j'aurais dû (faire)* 5.6
direct and indirect speech 8.12
direct object pronouns 6.2; 6.3
disjunctive pronouns 6.7
dont (of which, of whom, whose) 3.4

doubt: verbs of doubt + subjunctive 10.4
du, de la, de l', des 1.3; 7.1
du + masculine countries 1.6

E

each other (third person plural) 2.8
emphatic pronouns (moi, toi, lui, elle, nous, vous, eux, elles) 6.8
emotion 6.1
expressions of emotion using quel 6.1
expressions of emotion + subjunctive 8.7; 9.5
en + feminine countries 1.6
en + present participle 1.4
en + pronoun (some, of it, or them) 1.7; 6.5
en + time 1.8
enough + adjective (*assez riche*) 7.3
enough + noun (*assez d'argent*) 7.3
enough + infinitive (*assez riche pour...*) 7.3
everything (tout) 3.5
everybody (tout le monde) 3.5
expressions of quantity (*beaucoup de...*) 3.6; 7.1

F

fewer than + numbers 1.9
for + expressions of time 6.14
from + names of countries 1.6
future tense 4.1
future tense after quand, dès que... 4.2
future perfect tense 4.3

G

good contrasted with well 8.3

H

(he) had done: pluperfect tense 8.1
(to) help somebody to do something (aider-type verbs) 5.2

I

if: si + present, imperfect or pluperfect tense 7.5
il est or c'est? 5.8
imperative 5.3
imperfect tense 2.2; 3.9
impersonal phrases 5.8
impersonal verbs 5.8
in (after a superlative) 1.6; 3.3
in + area of a country (*in the south-east of France*) 1.6

in + names of countries 1.6
in + parts of the day 2.5
in + time (en or dans?) 1.8
indirect object pronouns 6.3; 6.4
indirect speech 8.12
infinitive constructions 1.5; 3.8; 4.4; 5.11; 5.12; 6.9; 9.6
infinitive after prepositions (pour, sans...) 1.5
interrogative adjectives 4.6; 6.1; 7.8
interrogative adverbs 4.6
adjectives + à + infinitive 4.4
adjectives + de + infinitive 4.4
nouns, quelque chose, rien + à + infinitive 6.9
noun phrases + de + infinitive (*avoir le temps de*) 4.4
verbs + infinitive (no preposition) 3.8; 4.4; 5.12; 9.6
verbs + à de + infinitive 5.1; 5.2
it (direct object pronoun): le, la 6.2
it is (c'est or il est?) 5.8
it is + noun (*c'est une bonne idée*) 5.8
it is + adjective + infinitive (*il est facile de...*) 5.8

J

jobs (omission of un or une) 4.9
jusqu'à ce que + subjunctive 10.4

K

(to) know how to do something:
savoir + infinitive 2.4

L

last (position of dernier) 5.7
le, la, les (pronouns) 6.2
le samedi (*on Saturdays*), le matin (*in the mornings*) 2.5
lequel, laquelle (des deux) 7.8
less than + numbers 7.1
leur, leurs (possessive adjectives) 6.11
lui, leur (pronouns) 6.4

M

(to) make + ajective (*to make life difficult*): rendre 9.4
mal contrasted with mauvais 8.3
many, much : beaucoup de 7.1
me, to me 6.3
le même...que (the same as) 2.7
mieux contrasted with meilleur 8.3
moins de + numbers 1.9
moins de + quantity 7.1
moins...que 2.6
à moins que + subjunctive 10.4
mon, ma, mes (possessive adjectives) 6.10

mon + feminine noun beginning with a vowel **6.10**
(the) most (adjective): superlative **3.2**
most (of) **7.1**

N

negatives: rien de, personne de + adjective **8.11**
negative phrases **9.2**
negative + de **7.1**
negative + subjunctive in relative clauses **10.4**
next (position of prochain) **5.7**
no + noun : pas de, ne...aucun(e) **7.1**; **9.2**
nobody **8.10**; **8.11**; **9.2**
no longer **9.2**
nothing **8.11**
nothing, nobody (as subject of the sentence) **8.10**
not as (*good*) as **2.6**
notre, nos **6.10**
nouns + à + infinitive **6.9**
nouns + de + infinitive **4.4**
nouns used as numbers (*une vingtaine*) **1.9**
nouveau, nouvel, nouvelle **6.13**
numbers **1.9**

O

on + days of the week **2.5**
on doing something (en + present participle) **1.4**
on + son, sa, ses; soi and vous **8.5**
one's (possessive adjective) : son, sa, ses **8.5**
(I) ought (to do): (je) devrais (faire) **5.6**
(I) ought (to have done): (j')aurais dû (faire) **5.6**

P

passive **9.1**
past historic **Appendix 3**
pendant contrasted with depuis and pour **6.14**
perfect infinitive **5.4**; **5.5**
perfect tense **3.7**
perfect or imperfect? **3.9**
perfect subjunctive **10.3**
perhaps **9.3**
personne as subject of sentence **8.10**
peut-être (perhaps) **9.3**
(la) plupart **7.1**
pluperfect tense **8.1**
plus de + numbers **1.9**
plus...que **2.6**
plusieurs (contrasted with quelques, certains) **7.2**

possessive adjectives 6.10
possessive pronouns 6.11
pour contrasted with pendant and depuis 6.14
pouvoir contrasted with savoir 2.4
pour que + subjunctive 10.4
pourvu que + subjunctive 10.4
prepositions **Appendix 1**
prepositions + infinitive 1.5
present participle 1.4
present tense 2.1
present subjunctive 10.2
prochain (position of) 5.7
pronouns: le, la, les 6.2
    lui, leur 6.4
    me, te, nous, vous 6.3
    y, en 6.5
pronouns used for emphasis 6.8
pronouns used with prepositions 6.7
pronouns: position of pronouns 6.6
pronouns with the infinitive 6.6
pronouns: double pronouns 6.6
pronouns with positive commands 5.2; 6.6
pronouns with negative commands 5.3

Q

quand + future tense 4.2
quantity expressions + de 3.6; 7.1
quel + noun in questions 4.6; 6.1; 7.8
quel + noun in exclamations 6.1
quelque chose + de + ajective 8.10
quelques (contrasted with certains, plusieurs) 7.2
quelqu'un + de + adjective 8.11
question forms 4.6
question words: comment? 4.6
qu'est-ce que? or que? 4.7
qu'est-ce qui? or qui? 4.7
quoi? 4.7
qui, que, dont 3.4
quoique + subjunctive 10.4

R

reflexive pronouns 2.2; 2.8
reflexive verbs in the present 2.2
reflexive verbs (use of se) 2.8
reflexive verbs in the infinitive 8.6
relative clauses using the subjunctive 10.4
relative pronouns: qui, que, dont 3.4
rendre (to make) + adjective 9.4
rien (as subject of sentence) 8.10

rien de + ajective **8.11**
rien + à + infinitive **6.9**

S

(the) same...as: le même...que **2.7**
sans que + subjunctive **10.4**
savoir contrasted with pouvoir **2.4**
se (each other) **2.8**
si (such) (*un si mauvais repas*) **8.9**
si (if) + present, imperfect or pluperfect tense **7.5**
si (if) shortened before il(s) **7.5**
(I) should (do): (je) devrais (faire) **5.6**
(I) should have (done): (J')aurais dû (faire) **5.6**
soi(-même) **8.5**
some, a few, several **7.2**
some + noun: du, de la, de l', des **7.1**
some (pronoun): en **6.5**
someone, something + adjective:
quelqu'un de (sympathique), quelque chose de (délicieux) **8.11**
subjunctive:
use of the subjunctive, general note **10.1**
present subjunctive **10.2**
perfect subjunctive **10.3**
use of subjunctive, detailed practive **10.4**
used with expressions of emotion **8.7; 9.5**
various uses of the subjunctive **10.4**
such a (problem): un tel (*problème*) **8.9**
such a (serious problem): un (*problème*) si (*sérieux*) **8.9**
superlative **3.2**
superlative form of adverbs **5.10**
superlative + relative clause in the subjunctive **3.3; 10.4**

T

tel, telle, tes, telles (*un tel problème*) **8.9**
tenses:
present **2.1**
future **4.1**
conditional **7.4**
imperfect **2.3; 3.9**
perfect **3.7; 3.9**
pluperfect **8.1**
present subjunctive **10.2**
perfect subjunctive **10.3**
their (possessive adjective): leur, leurs **6.10**
there: y **6.5**
this, that, these, those **7.6**
the one(s) who/which **7.7**
time expressions: depuis, pendant, pour; dans, en **1.8; 6.14**
to: to him, to her, to them **6.4**

to: to + names of countries 1.6
too + adjective – trop (paresseux) 7.3
+ infinitive – trop (paresseux) pour (apprendre) 7.3
+ infinitive – trop de (travail) 7.3
tous: all, everyone (pronoun) 3.5
tout: everything (pronoun) 3.5
tout, toute, tous, toutes: all, every (adjective) 3.5
tout le monde: everybody 3.5
trop + adjective: *trop (paresseux)* 7.3
trop de + noun: *trop de travail* 7.3
trop + infinitive: *trop (paresseux) pour (apprendre)* 7.3

U

une, une omitted with jobs, professions 4.9
un, une used in adverbial phrases (*avec une rapidité étonnante*) 5.9

V

venir de + infinitive 3.8
verbs + à + infinitive 3.8; 9.6
verbs + à + person + de + infinitive (*demander*-type verbs) 5.1; 5.2
verbs + de + infinitive 9.6
verbs + infinitive 5.11; 5.12; 9.6
verbs + person + à + infinitive (*aider*-type verbs) 5.1; 5.2
verbs + à + person (*donner, montrer*...) 8.8
verbs: reflexive verbs 2.2; 2.8; 8.6
vieux, vieil, vieille (*un vieil ami*) 6.13
votre, vos (possessive adjectives) 6.10
vouloir que + subjunctive 8.7; 10.4

W

(to) want someone to do something: vouloir que + subjunctive 8.7; 10.4
was (in passive): (he was killed) 9.1
well contrasted with badly 8.3
what (in direct questions):
qu'est-ce qui? 4.7
qu'est-ce que? 4.7
...quoi? 4.7
what (in direct questions): ce qui, ce que, ce dont 4.7
what/which + noun (interrogative) 4.7
what + noun (exclamation) 4.7
when: quand + future 4.2
which (referring back to an idea): ce qui, ce que 4.7
which one(s)?: lequel, laquelle, lesquels, lesquelles 7.8
while (doing something): en + present participle 1.4
who, whom, which (relative pronoun): qui, que 3.4
whose, of whom: dont 3.4

Y

y: there, to it (pronoun replacing à + place) 6.5